ATHENIAN
RED FIGURE VASES
The Archaic Period
a handbook

JOHN BOARDMAN

528 illustrations

THAMES AND HUDSON

© *1975 Thames and Hudson Ltd, London*
Reprinted 1993

ISBN 0–500–20143–9

Printed and bound in Singapore by C.S. Graphics

University, then Professor. He has excavated in Crete, Chios and Libya. His other handbooks are devoted to *Greek Sculpture* (volumes on the Archaic and the Classical), *Athenian Black Figure Vases* and *Athenian Red Figure Vases: The Classical Period*. He is also the author of *Greek Art* in the World of Art series; excavation publications; *The Greeks Overseas*; *The Parthenon and its Sculptures*; and several books on ancient gems and finger rings.

WORLD OF ART

This famous series
provides the widest available
range of illustrated books on art in all its aspects.
If you would like to receive a complete list
of titles in print please write to:
THAMES AND HUDSON
30 Bloomsbury Street, London WC1B 3QP
In the United States please write to:
THAMES AND HUDSON INC.
500 Fifth Avenue, New York, New York 10110

Printed in Singapore

Calyx crater signed by Euphronios. Death and Sarpedon. See 22

CONTENTS

Chapter One

INTRODUCTION

The red figure technique of vase painting was invented in Athens by about 530 B C at a time when the black figure technique was barely past its prime and when several other important studios of vase painting were flourishing in the Greek world, from the western colonies to Ionia. At the end of the half century or more discussed in this book, Athenian red figure stood alone as the only major figure-decorated style of vase painting in Greece, and its painters had posed and solved problems in draughtsmanship which were beyond even the imagination of earlier artists. That this affected the status of the painter in society seems likely to judge from what we can learn of the Pioneers. In Athens the only competitor was black figure, which remained plentiful, but declined in quality rapidly after 500 and is no longer worth consideration after 470 except on Panathenaic vases.

Although Athens, especially in the fine though fragmentary dedications from the Acropolis, remains a prime source for red figure, the export trade, notably to Italy, has ensured for us the greatest number of complete vases, which are therefore to be sought in the museums of Italy and the West rather than Greece itself. The very wide distribution, far beyond the Greek world, has meant that the pottery, with the possibilities of its close dating, offers historical evidence of great importance for non-Classical cultures, and is also a good indicator of the Athenian pottery trade or other Athenian interests. Here and there in this book these matters are touched upon, but the main attractions of the study are the insight it gives to the operation of a community of crafts-men in a major Greek city, the information of historical, social and mytho-logical value given by the figure scenes, and, not least, the intrinsic quality of the work of the finer artists. The black figure artist Exekias (working about 545–530) had raised the craft of vase painting to the status of a major art, and so, in the hands of some, it remained through the Archaic period until over-taken by the art of painters on wood or wall.

It is these interests and quality which this volume seeks to document and discuss for the student, connoisseur of ancient art or lover of fine drawing. It is a sequel to the handbook on Athenian black figure vases (*ABFH*) which was published in 1974, and attempts in the same way to provide a text which describes the development of style as well as offering some guide to understanding and enjoying the figure scenes. Some matters have been dealt with already in *ABFH* and need be only briefly rehearsed here. The pictures are plentiful, though small, chosen to illustrate style, shapes and decoration as fully as possible. For a fuller appreciation of the finer vases the reader must turn to life-size or enlarged photographs in the more expensive art books, or to the vases themselves in public collections. I have used drawings of vases where some details or whole scenes are better presented this way, including several of Beazley's, hitherto unpublished, where the thickened pencil lines can indicate use of 'relief line' contour missed in photographs. Some of the older drawings used are convenient but may be defective in detail. Most figures and scenes on vases cannot be caught complete and without distortion in a single camera shot. This is no serious fault of design since in life eyes and hands can move to help present the whole pictures.

The content of this book covers the Archaic period, down to the 470's, with a short sequel following some Archaic styles into the Early Classical. These chapters inevitably rely heavily on the writings of Sir John Beazley who, on his death in 1970, had earned an international reputation and authority in this subject unrivalled in the history of Classical scholarship. I have seldom deviated from the order of his lists or hesitatingly queried conclusions which he was himself always ready to revise in the light of new evidence or experience. There is no place for dogma in Classical archaeology, for clinging to con-venient assertions, or to the slick art-historical generalisations which may satisfy the student more readily than they satisfy the evidence. The subject moves too quickly. No small part of Beazley's brilliance was his humility: but he suffered fools not at all.

The principles of attribution of vases to painters were demonstrated by Beazley in several of his earlier articles, from 1910 on, based on methods applied to Italian painting by Morelli and other nineteenth-century scholars. It depends on observation and comparison of details – anatomy, dress – which, combined with study of pose, composition and the indefinable 'style', makes attribution of the more idiosyncratic artists possible even for beginners. How objective is this? It might not satisfy the new archaeologist, but we need not be ashamed that we can use our eyes as effectively as our instruments. The coherence of a group of vases attributed to one hand by Beazley can be demon-strated by computer analysis of detail (albeit subjectively chosen) but the pain of recording the tens of thousands of Athenian vases for a computer to detect the painters would not be justified by the results, although it can be done for a single monument with repetitive figures by different hands (as in the Persepolis reliefs, where the eye could achieve the same results yet quicker).

There are other special problems in the study of red figure potter work, where more mechanical comparisons might be possible. Potter signatures help, and the study of profile details pioneered by Professor Bloesch. The relationships of potter to painter, and the criteria by which master/pupil or workshop relationships may be defined are sometimes clear, sometimes not. Beazley found it necessary to point out that he made 'a distinction between a vase by a painter and a vase in his manner; and that "manner", "imitation", "following", "school", "circle", "group", "influence", "kinship", are not, in my vocabulary, synonyms.' Not all students will be able to follow all these distinctions.

Where the later work attributed to a painter shows some coarsening of definition, is this an indication of the failing eyesight of middle age, or the work of a pupil or imitator? Euphronios, the young painter, in later years worked only as potter. And was moved to make a dedication for good health on the Acropolis. This we can judge from inscriptions. Did others put down their brushes less readily? At any rate, who was the more important in a workshop, painter or potter? It is the potter who requires the permanent installation of a kiln for his work, and no doubt many or most artists could practise both crafts.

A further point, referred to intermittently in this book and in *ABFH*, may be mentioned here: the possible non-Athenian contribution to the development of red figure in Athens. Some debt to Ionia might seem plausible in the light of East Greek influence in other arts, but stylistically it is impossible to prove, except in the matter of the maeander and square patterns which had a very long history in East Greece, are met in Athenian black figure rarely, but only appear regularly in red figure from about 500, as we shall see. The palmette patterns seem equally elusive. The role of the metic population in the artistic life of Athens seems generally admitted, but we cannot point to any single painter whose training does not seem to be thoroughly Athenian, although the mood of some with foreign names (as Skythes) seems to indicate a fresh approach. Attempts to show that the Kleophrades Painter was a Corinthian, on grounds of style alone, are unlikely to be convincing. Spelling could prove more interesting – the ionicising Goluchow Painter, spelling oddities by Phintias (who can Atticise his name to Philtias) or the Brygos Painter ('p' for 'ph' like the Scythian in Aristophanes). The names are in themselves suggestive and, taken all together, effectively counter arguments based on the proven use of foreign names in a few Greek noble families. We have some hundred and twenty-five names of potters and painters on vases studied in *ABFH* and this book. Of these a half at least bear names which are decidedly not appropriate to Athenian families of upper or lower (so far as can be judged) class. Some name another land or race – Lydos, Skythes, Sikanos, Sikelos, Syriskos, Kolchos, Thrax, Kares, Mys: others bear names appropriate elsewhere or derived from foreign names – e.g. Amasis, Brygos, Midas, Phintias, Ismenos, Makron and the Herm– names commonest in East Greece; several seem nicknames or adopted names – Epiktetos ('new acquired' – a slave name), Pistoxenos ('trusty foreigner' = Syriskos), Euenporos ('good trader'), Onesimos ('profitable'), Paidikos ('boy mad'), Priapos, Smikros (Tiny), Oreibelos ('mountain-goer'). But it is hard to categorise, and these are samples

9

only. This is not the place to attempt individual explanations, nor is enough yet known about how and when metics or slaves might acquire or change their names, except that it was easier for them than for citizens. Look at the list of kalos names from the same vases, where you find hardly a single name of this type, to judge the difference in status and origins between the artisans and their cynosures.

This is a period for which, for the first time in Greek art, we may have literary references to the work and styles of painters – not vase painters but wall painters. The main influence of the great muralists on vase painting is later than Archaic, but there are a few late comments on their predecessors. Pliny says that before Polygnotos, therefore Late Archaic, the painter Kimon of Kleonai introduced foreshortening and three-quarter faces (if Pliny understood the term aright, and if we understand Pliny) and realistic touches in dress and anatomy (veins). The sort of true foreshortening of whole limbs which a later critic would have noticed is not characteristic of Archaic red figure, so either the vase painters were falling short of Kimon's achievement or we date Kimon rather too early. He was supposed to have improved on the work of Eumaros, an Athenian in whom some have seen Eumares, father of Antenor, an Athenian sculptor who worked about 530–510. Lacking any record of major wall paintings of these years in Athens we cannot pretend that any mural style was yet influential. But recent discoveries of Archaic Greek painting in tombs in Italy (Paestum [1.1]) and Lycia (Elmali [1.2]), should warn us that it is in this medium, with larger figures and the greater realism of a pale background, that we should expect major advances in composition to be achieved. It is to a different art, however, that we shall turn for an explanation of the inception of red figure itself.

Red figure cup fragment photographed in reflected light to show the painted outline to the figure, the 'relief line' contour and hip, and thinned paint for other anatomical details

Chapter Two

THE FIRST GENERATION

The red figure technique

For nearly one hundred years all the figure decoration on Athenian pottery had been executed in the 'black figure' technique. This meant black-painted silhouettes with incised linear detail and added red and white for details of hair, dress or female flesh. The technique had satisfied Corinth for even longer, but it was in many ways restrictive and in other parts of Greece, notably the islands and seventh-century Attica, outline drawn figures were preferred, often picked out with broad masses of colour. It was probably Corinth's trading successes with her pottery which ensured that black figure would prevail, but the outline drawn styles were by no means forgotten. The finest of the Athenian black figure artists were at work in the third quarter of the sixth century. They achieved the heights, and the limits, of what the technique could offer. Progress was impossible, decline inevitable, and this is made clear by the following half century of black figure. But this did not mean the end of figure painting on vases since by about 530 BC an alternative technique, 'red figure', was invented in Athens, and this revitalised the craft. Unlike black figure this was an essentially Athenian achievement – virtually all the figure-decorated vases in the Greek world of the fifth and fourth centuries are Athenian red figure, but for the Athens-inspired South Italian schools which start work in the second half of the fifth century.

To the viewer the effect of the change is readily seized. Red figure is the reverse of black figure. Figures and patterns are reserved in the colour of the red clay ground with linear detail painted upon them and the background filled in with black, where before the background was plain, the detail incised and the figures black. The process may probably be best understood by describing the preparation of a red figure vase, before we turn to the advantages and limitations of the technique, and its origins. The potter hands over the vase to the painter in a dried, leather-hard, near brittle condition, but still unfired. The painter may then sketch the outlines of the intended decoration on the surface with a blunt instrument which leaves light furrows, or possibly charcoal which would burn out in the firing. These are subsequently covered by paint or surface preparation but the furrows are generally still detectable

[5] and often give evidence for poses or compositions altered in the painting. The outlines are then drawn in a line or band of black paint, then the details of the figures, leaving any minor touches of added colour for the end, and the background is filled in. Florals and border patterns will already have been allowed for, and the pot is ready for firing.

The ordinary black-brown gloss paint was not very effective when fine lines were required, because it was fairly runny and in a fine line so little sat on the vase that the result was pale brown or honey-coloured, not black. This had troubled black figure artists too, and soon after the mid sixth century a different mixture of paint and means of applying it were invented to produce a 'relief line' of intense black which stood proud of the vase surface. The black figure artists used this to divide the tongues of decorative friezes and for spears or staffs. The red figure artists used it, hesitantly at first, sharpening the outlines of figures (where many black figure artists incised), since otherwise the thinner paint did not always leave a clearly defined edge, and for anatomical or dress details. But they soon also recognised the value of what had been the fault of the thinner paint and they used it still for minor linear details, picking out their figures in lines of varying intensity, as well as areas of wash or mottled effects on animal skins. (See the fig. on p. 10.)

Relief line is so important in early red figure that, although potting techniques are not described in this volume, a word about it is called for. Scholars have long speculated about how the relief line was made since the slip paint must have been very thick and not easy to run off a brush. It can be seen that the line often starts solid, ends with a longitudinal groove. This surely implies a heavy bristle tip, well fed by most carefully prepared slip paint. When full the line is solid; emptying, the bristle has no paint on its upper edge to fill in behind the line drawn by the tip. Mr Noble, to whom we owe much in the elucidation and demonstration of Greek potting techniques, suggested that a syringe device of some sort was used. But Greek technical artistry is characterised by trouble, not tricks. The nozzle would require very difficult co-ordination of pressure and movement and cannot explain the relief-to-groove phenomenon satisfactorily. Nor is it easy to believe that black figure artists had invented such an instrument merely to draw pattern borders and spears, or that it had value in any other craft.

There were other obvious advantages in the new technique. The black figure graver may have been easier to use than a brush for miniaturist detail, but in all other respects the brush offered greater freedom. The figures were now lifelike, or at least closer to life than the unrealistic black, and against a black ground they stood sharply defined on the vase. In other arts the claims of pattern and of anatomical plausibility were becoming more easily reconciled but the uncompromising two-dimensional quality of black figure, juxtaposing frontal and profile parts of the body, could not accommodate the new interest as effectively as brushwork, especially when lines of different

12

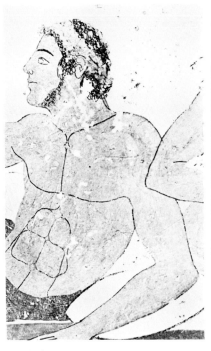

1.1 Tomb painting at Paestum

1.3 Painted stele from Sunium

1.2 Tomb painting at Elmali

1.4 Siphnian Treasury frieze at Delphi

intensity could be used. The limitations of the new technique were not, however, inconsiderable. The simple black = male, white = female, sex differentiation was gone and details of dress or hair style do not always prove decisive, while there was a tendency to depict gods and heroes as younger and so beardless. There was some initial difficulty through not allowing for the thickness of the contour line, lost to the figure when the background is filled in, and this produces some unduly skinny fingers. With no colour and less pattern compositions of overlapping figures would be confusing, so there is a tendency to keep figures apart. These were all limitations apparent to the painter, which he faced and overcame in different ways. Another, not apparent to him, was the effect of the black ground which removed all possibility of rendering depth of field and which, in this craft, meant that even the simplest perspective was not attempted. The figures stand spot-lighted on a narrow stage. Muralists of the Classical period were not hampered in this way because they used a white background and in their work lay the possibilities of progress, but their paintings have not survived except in ancient reports or Roman copies. In the sixth century there may have been less divergence between the appearance of black figure and major painting, so far as we can judge. Red figure represents a positive break with painting traditions, and was differently inspired, as we shall see.

Outline drawing in vase painting had been practised intermittently in sixth-century Athens, most recently by the Amasis Painter, but the appearance of outlined figures against a black ground was new, although there are a few mid-seventh-century Cretan vases which anticipate the effect in a primitive way. It might be enough to explain the new figures in terms of simple plausibility – flesh is pale red rather than black, but to explain the dark background we have to look no further than a cognate art form always closely linked with that of line drawing and possibly practised by the same artists – relief sculpture. It was common practice for the relief backgrounds to be painted dark red or blue, leaving the figures in the white marble, with only features or drapery picked out in washes of colour. Red figure minus the added colours gives the same effect. Shallow relief sculpture was popular in Athens, notably on the grave stelai, and it was coming to occupy more important positions on buildings. Some of it is hardly more than careful line drawing rendered in low relief, and on a few stelai where the figures are only painted the dark background is kept, as for the reliefs [1.3]. On the Siphnian Treasury at Delphi we have preserved extensive parts of four relief friezes which can be closely dated to little before 525 BC and give an excellent idea of the figure work which can readily be matched on the earliest red figure vases [1.4]. The comparison with sculpture may go deeper, however, and it might be fair to read in some of the conventions of red figure more conscious imitation of relief work. Thus, much of the linear detail in red figure seems to indicate contour rather than to delimit areas: what the black figure artist would define in straight intersecting boundaries the red figure artist renders in rounded outlines. Obvious examples are the treatment of stomach muscles, or the minor muscles around knees and on legs, or the use of hook motifs for collar bones or ankles, which again defined relief masses and had been used sparingly by black figure artists. We might have expected some attempts at shading to render relief, but this appears only rarely and in a very rudimentary form (between Antaios' stomach muscles on [23], or by the shield rim on [268]). When palmette leaves, however, begin to show a centre rib, the effect is to make them look more like the relief anthemia of gravestone or architecture, and when a centre palmette leaf is allowed to overlap its encircling tendril [39.1] the three-dimensional effect is heightened. Closer observation of anatomy patterns had been a progressive characteristic of sixth-century sculpture, no less practised in relief work where more ambitious poses and compositions could be executed than in free standing works. The draughtsman of red figure seizes and exploits these new trends in a way denied the black figure artist, and in some respects he seems even to lead, since it is on vases that we first see that accurate observation of the effect on a body of the shift of weight on to one leg which, in the early fifth century, is to be a hallmark of the sculptor's graduation from the Archaic to the Early Classical. So we can observe here the development of a craft which was to be in the vanguard at an important period of transition in Greek art. It is fortunate for the historian that artists of distinction chose at this time to ply their trade in the Athens potters' quarter.

Invention and Experiment

The ANDOKIDES PAINTER (working c. 530–515) is the first known practitioner of the full red figure technique, named for the potter for whom he worked. From his hand [2–10] we have at least fourteen amphorae and two cups, and half of these also display the black figure technique – six amphorae are 'bilingual', one side red figure, one side black figure [2]; another has black figure (on a white ground) on the lip [6]; one cup exterior shares techniques, the other is black figure only within. The black figure work can be recognised on a number of other wholly black figure vases attributed by Beazley to the Lysippides Painter (ABFH figs. 163, 165–6). He changed his mind more than once about whether in fact two artists or only one was involved, deciding finally for two, but this is a solution which many other scholars have found it difficult to accept. One general argument against it is that the first red figure painter could hardly have started his career with the new technique, and the earliest red figure by our painter is so very much a simple negative of black figure that he must have been a black figure painter by training, rather than, say, a muralist who would probably have worked on a pale background and without incising detail. The difficulty arises when comparisons are attempted between similar scenes executed in the two techniques. Three of the bilingual amphorae present virtually the same scene on each side. On the Boston amphora with Herakles and a bull the correspondence is close: [8] and *ABFH* fig. *164*. On the other vases the differences are so great that either a different hand was at work, or our artist was very deliberately covering his traces and demonstrating differences. The red figure on other bilinguals so closely matches the black figure of the 'Lysippides Painter' (*ABFH* figs. *162–3*) that identity seems assured; so the Andokides Painter did paint black figure, but did he paint all the black figure on his bilingual vases? As in all such problems of attribution the answer lies in study of detail and in study of theme and composition. On the latter score identity is almost total – similar preoccupation with certain Herakles scenes and similar treatment of them (new ways with the lion, especially kneeling, lying or throwing [7, *10*]; with Kerberos; feasting with Athena: *ABFH* figs. *161–3*). With the details of drawing the answer is less clear. Many features are alike – helmets, trees, animals, ornaments – but the minor anatomical details which so often prove decisive in attribution present problems. Knee caps are favoured for display of pattern. On the black figures they are rendered usually as a swelling Cupid's-bow shape: on the red figures by two long hooks [5, 9]. But on [8] the red figure knee resembles the black figure and when we reflect on the difference of technique the divergence is explained. In black figure there was no great difficulty in scratching a single

short line changing direction of curve four times. With a stiff brush it was almost impossible, hence the fragmentation of the pattern into two long hooks which also more closely resembled the treatment of muscles above and below the cap in relief sculpture. Once the solution was found both types could appear on one vase. Then look at ears. The black figure ears show lobe and antitragus as two full curves. There is the same problem of technique in red figure, so, although the area of the long lobe is the same, the division is usually omitted or barely hinted at [3] while the inner markings of the ear are rendered in short lines. This may all seem an exercise in trivialities but no excuse is required for trying to establish the identity and achievement of the inventor of red figure, and these are criteria on which painter attribution is based.

The ornament on the vases is all still black figure and the influence of the older technique is seen in the lavish use of pattern on dress, the amount of added red, and free use of incision to outline black areas of hair. From the start the saucer eyes of black figure men are replaced by the unisex almond shape, but still frontal, with the pupil barely shifted towards the front. The Andokides Painter is uncertain about how much use to make of anatomical details. Much he omits, yet on the New York amphora, one of the earliest, we see the fully patterned treatment of the stomach. Dress falls to S-curving hems, not the tight zigzag folds of later red figure, and he is not yet sure about letting the body contours show through. The dressed males are still close to the drawing of the black figure master Exekias in whom we may recognise the Andokides Painter's teacher. He copies some of his subjects too, such as the Ajax and Achilles playing: [2] and *ABFH* fig. *100*. We might wonder what part Exekias played in the invention of red figure. He was an innovator in techniques and shapes, but his black figure never drops into outline drawing as readily as that of some of his contemporaries, and technical innovation need not go hand in hand with high artistry.

The Andokides Painter's themes show less a change in subject than in mood with fuller emphasis on individual figures. They range from traditional myth, novelties like Herakles holding a bundle of spits and driving a bull to sacrifice [8], to genre scenes like the Baigneuses of [4]. These are drawn exceptionally over a prepared white ground not the red clay alone. He used white ground for black figures on the lip of the New York amphora [6], but here the bodies are themselves more as they would have appeared in black figure or the Six technique for all that they are reserved in the new manner.

If comparisons between the Siphnian Treasury friezes [1.4] and his work are just he should have started painting red figure about 530. Apart from the Budapest cup [5], which is early, most of his bilinguals are later (about 520) with a more conscious demonstration of the rival styles dramatically juxtaposed on the Palermo cup, where the technique changes in mid figure (*ABFH* fig. *160*), between body and shield.

There are other bilinguists and innovators to be considered here. PSIAX [11–15] signs two alabastra made by Hilinos and his hand is recognised on other vases including amphorae made by the potter Andokides (a bilingual [14]) and Menon. He shows more interest in smaller shapes. His career begins in the 520's; the red figure is already beyond the experimental and showing figure contour through dress with less emphasis on colour or pattern. The floral patterns on his vases are still black figure, or earliest red figure with fan palmettes and spiky lotuses [12]. His work in the two techniques is closely matched, the incised lines in black figure being brittle and finicky. He was a late convert to red figure and decorates a black figure neck amphora for Andokides, but with the figures confined to the neck, the body black, in what might be regarded as the new style. The black figure work (*ABFH* figs. *168–71*) has something of the febrile elegance of the Amasis Painter, whom Beazley thought might have been his teacher, but the effect is partly due to his conscious attempt to translate some of the new red figure manners into the older technique. In red figure he was better at dress than anatomy, overdoing the belly contouring for his falling warrior on [15] and quite failing the three-quarter view though he tries to twist the trailing foot to a frontal aspect. He is free with incision for hair and weapons, and uses added white for some details like tails or wreaths, and added clay relief for a bow string. He used a white ground in black figure work and practised the Six technique (see *ABFH* p. 106): it is his white ground vases which indicate that he was painting still in about 510/500. He may not have stayed with red figure to the end. His range of subjects is unambitious – Dionysiac, Apolline, warriors in action or leaving home, with a fondness for archers [*12, 13*].

Another important bilinguist is PASEAS (formerly called the Kerberos Painter), whose *floruit* is 520–510 [*16, 17*]. His red figure work, mainly on cups and plates, is canonical for cup painters of the period, with neat, rather big-headed figures, their eyes often narrow, set high forwards, and he shows a residual interest in colour and pattern. This shows well on the Boston plate [*16*] which gave him his sobriquet before his true name was discovered (*ABFH* p. 106), or on the Oxford plate where Miltiades is praised (the letters escape the camera) and where scholars have sought to associate the mounted archer in northern dress [*17*] with the younger Miltiades, later victor at Marathon, who in these years was operating in Thrace. Miltiades is only named as kalos here, but he was no longer a youth and this is not Thracian dress, although it might have passed as such in Athens. Paseas' black figure is on white ground plaques made for dedication on the Acropolis (*ABFH* fig. *172*) and it is for his colour work and relationship to Psiax that he is named here. On a red figure plaque he uses white ground also, not, as the Andokides Painter did, for all the figures, but just for the women who are being made love to vigorously by men whose flesh is left in the natural red. The subject may seem odd for a dedicatory plaque, yet it recurs on one from the Acropolis [*18*], where the same white-red sex colouring is used, but the background is not blacked in and it is somewhat later. This extreme colour realism did not, apparently, catch on, but it is undeniably effective where the sex contrast, as in these scenes, is significant and exciting.

We might have expected more experiment with purely outline drawing on a red or white ground, but extensive use of this technique is to be reserved for the fifth century. From the early years of red figure there is a cup in Adolphseck [*19*] which offers simple outline in the very earliest red figure manner on the outside, an ordinary black figure gorgoneion within, and rather later the Gotha cup [*51*] has outlined figures on white ground outside and Pioneer red figure within. Stray experiments appear on an Acropolis cup fragment with red figure, the background coral-red instead of black (and so a parallel use to that with black figure in Exekias' famous cup, *ABFH* fig. *104.3*), and a plaque where white ground is used in a similar manner.

2.1, 2 Belly amphora (Type A) by the Andokides Painter. Ajax and Achilles play

3.1–3 *Belly amphora (Type A) by the Andokides Painter*

4 Belly amphora (Type A) by the Andokides Painter. White ground figures

Preliminary sketch

5.1–3 Cup by the Andokides Painter

6 Belly amphora (Type A) by the Andokides Painter. White ground lip

7 Belly amphora (Type A) by the Andokides Painter. Herakles and the Lion

8 Belly amphora (Type A) by the Andokides Painter. Herakles drives a bull to sacrifice. H. 53·3

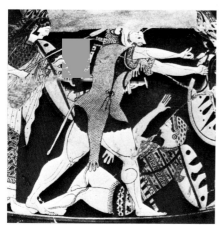

9.1 Belly amphora (Type A) by the Andokides
Painter. Herakles and Amazons

9.2 Reverse of 9.1

10 Belly amphora (Type A) by the Andokides Painter. Herakles and the Lion

11 Belly amphora (Type A) by Psiax. Dionysos at feast

12 Alabastron signed by Psiax

13 Cup by Psiax

14.1, 2 Belly amphora (Type A) by Psiax.
Artemis; Satyr and Dionysos

15 Cup by Psiax

16 Plate by Paseas. Herakles and Kerberos. W. 18·9

17 Plate by Paseas

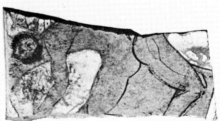

18 Votive plaque. W. 7·3

19 Cup. Dionysos

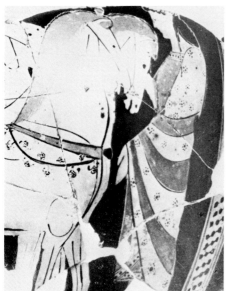

20 Column crater

21 Oinochoe by the
Goluchow Painter. H. 21

Finally, there are various examples of primitive red figure [20], some on bilingual vases otherwise decorated as ordinary late sixth-century black figure. The GOLUCHOW PAINTER is placed here by Beazley, rightly I think, for the crude anatomy of his figures on oinochoai [21] and use of colour, although the poses seem to owe something to the Pioneers, and some scholars prefer a later date for his work. He uses two alphabets on his vases – Attic, and Ionian of the Cyclades – a circumstance worth a moment's thought. Much else in Athens of these years – relief sculpture, architecture – is demonstrably affected by the work of Ionian or island artists, and we have the evidence of inscribed bases on the Acropolis for their physical presence in Athens. There had been intermittent influence on vase painting too through the sixth century. Is red figure another of the gifts from the East? It was certainly not invented there, and its debt to Attic black figure conventions is perfectly clear. The cosmopolitan character of the Athens potters' quarter seems revealed in borrowed shape or ornament rather than any positive influence on style and in Athens the vase painting tradition was, by 530, too strongly rooted and indeed dominant in the Greek world to accommodate much radical change of foreign inspiration. If we may suspect or even prove non-Athenian blood in some of the artists (see Chapter One) this need not make us look for anything significantly foreign in their art.

The Pioneers

The painters of the Pioneer Group are possibly the most interesting of all that worked in the Athens potters' quarter not merely for their artistic merits, but for their character and coherence as a group. It is as though, for the first time in the history of Western art, we can here discern a conscious movement, a camaraderie of artists. Since we know no more about them than we can learn from their vases, with not a scrap of help from any ancient writer, the reconstruction of their careers, common purpose, even rivalries, can be taken as a triumph of archaeological research, though there are many archaeologists who might not recognise it as such.

The peculiarities which mark them out from their predecessors, and many of their successors, are readily defined. They were consummate artists. If Beazley calls Smikros 'not a good draughtsman' this is true only in the context of the group. Although their earliest work comes only about a decade after the invention of red figure it must be remembered that the inventors and experimenters, presented in the last section, were still at work, but while they were making progress in the 'mechanics' of the new technique, the Pioneers had seized upon the essence of what red figure could offer, refining it in detail of drawing and composition, to achieve a quality of mood and narrative which went far beyond what a Psiax or Paseas could conceive, and which was carried on only piecemeal by different artists in the succeeding generation. They preferred painting big vases, all varieties of craters, the Type A amphorae, psykters, hydriai, but also decorated cups and plates, as well at home with the vignette as with the broad canvas. They were literate and garrulous. They signed their works freely, identified the guests in the symposia they depicted, threw in mottoes and challenges, even let their figures speak in modern cartoon style. 'As never Euphronios' ('hos oudepote Euphronios') boasts Euthymides on [33.2] beside one of his more ambitious anatomical studies of man in motion, and we are at once introduced to an atmosphere of Left Bank rivalry. Euthymides was a proud man, and to his signature sometimes adds the name of his father, Pollias, certainly the sculptor whose name is found on bases from the Acropolis. Euthymides himself is greeted on two unattributed vases of the Group ('chaireto Euthymides'; 'Euthymides chaire') and a woman drinker on a vase by Phintias toasts him ('soi tendi Euthymidei kaloi' [38.1]). On the same vase a young man holding a lyre is labelled Euthymides [38.2]. In the circumstances it seems wrong to reject identification, but we must not expect portraiture. Smikros was a painter of the Group – unfortunately his name was a common one but he identifies himself as a drinker on one of his own vases [32.2], so it should be the same man at the party drawn by Euphronios and similarly named [head details, left]. Smikros is named too in an obscure motto (apparently recording a comment by him) on a vase near Euphronios, and he is designated kalos on another. The Group share interest and admiration of the young beauties of the day – Philiades, Antias, and especially Leagros for whom one of Euphronios' drinking girls spins a cup: 'tin tande latasso [=latageo] Leagre' [27 left]. The family of Leagros, the darling of the Group, lived in the deme Kerameis, so the lad may have been a familiar figure at parties in the potters' quarter. With a 'Smikros kalos' may we take it that some of our artists were of the same fashionable set? A Phayllos is named among the athletes on two vases by Euthymides, one by Phintias, and on two others (one by Euphronios?) – surely the famous Phayllos of Kroton who fought at Salamis and won three victories in the Pythian Games, and was well enough known in Athens to have a statue on the Acropolis. Sosias was a potter for the Group and a Sosias or Sosis is named on vases by Phintias, Euthymides and others. A Sosias too is named as a bugger on a vase graffito found in the Agora in Athens, but the accidents of survival have spared us the necessity to restore the name of the accuser as Euphronios, and at any rate the graffito seems satisfactorily later.

There are some common features of style which can be taken as indicative of the best painting of the years about 520–500 and can conveniently be summarised. Some apply equally now to the contemporary cup painters, yet to be discussed. The Pioneers have lost most interest in colour and only Euphronios shows much concern still with pattern on dress, in the spirit of the Andokides Painter or of black figure. But relief blobs for hair ringlets, grapes and florals in figure scenes are used on some of the finer vases, and Euphronios and Euthymides have coral-red bands on their cups. The incising of hair contours is dying out and the use of relief line established for most outlines on finer vases and the bolder anatomical or dress marking. Euthymides uses – almost over-uses – the thin paint for most anatomical effects. In the dress the contrast of thinned and relief lines is well exploited, the close-set thin wavy lines for the upper part of chitons being regular, but Euthymides uses thinned lines also beside the heavier folds of himatia and skirts. The zigzag hemlines of dress are rendered in more realistic S-curves without losing any of the decorative effect of stacked or splaying folds. The further hemline, seen from inside, is usually a plain scalloped curve or series of curves. Eyes drop towards the tear duct, occasionally opening slightly here, and the round pupil is set at the centre, or just forward of centre. Eyelashes are *de rigueur* on the finest work. Varieties of pose are a matter of individual invention. Suffice it to observe that the Pioneers make their figures do what they will, unhampered by the technique and con-ventions which dictated the rigidity of the doll-like stiff-jointed black figures of earlier in the century. In their work we see how in simple line drawing a twisting view of front or back torso [*33.2*] can be rendered plausibly, how muscle patterns can even be foreshortened in a rudimentary way to heighten this effect. Whole limbs, however, are rendered at full length, whether profile, frontal, or in an attempted three-quarter, and there is no true linear fore-shortening of limbs, although by totally obscuring the shin or thigh in reclining figures, and showing top or under views of feet, the artist goes some way in suggesting the third dimension: e.g. [*27, 29, 51.1*]. There is something more close to proper linear foreshortening in the rendering of objects like shields. In the new convention for standing figures, suggesting a three-quarter or turning view with one leg in profile, one frontal, we have (especially where the profile leg is relaxed) an anticipation of what free standing sculpture will attempt only a generation later (in the 'Critian boy'). Look at Euphronios' figure [*24.1* left] and see how he is beginning to observe the shift of hips and torso which such a pose demands. Again we see a link between line drawing and sculpture, this time with sculpture in the round of a later date, and may speculate on what other arts these men may have practised.

In the circumstances it is odd to observe their continuing dilemma over the attachment of a profile head to a frontal torso: and especially over drawing a girl's breast in front view, a problem which the meanest latter-day wall-graffitist solves successfully with a circle and dot. The vase painters are obsessed still with the profile view, and when both breasts are shown they may point the same way [*27, 38.1*], or outwards [*38.1*], or downwards, or – the last indignity – inwards.

Floral pattern offers no great variety. Euthymides and Phintias still use some old black figure lotus and palmette chains [*40.2*], the lotuses totally emaciated, and thin bud and flower friezes. Black open palmettes in scrolls, circumscribed or one-up one-down, are commoner. The red figure florals, similarly arranged (but not one-up one-down) have open palmettes. There are few other varieties, some of which recall architectural patterns – palmettes in hearts (Euthymides), lyre-shaped scrolls (Euphronios, Pezzino Group). The Sosias Painter palmettes (quite late) have pointed leaves [50]. Centre leaves do not overlap their tendrils (Phintias does, once [39.1]). Euphronios gives us the red figure lotus with sharp outer petals and a sword-like centre leaf with two-leaf palmettes to fill [22], but Euthymides' lotuses are less compact. Lotus by now is a misnomer, but cup painters will leave botanical accuracy yet farther behind.

EUPHRONIOS [22–30, Frontispiece] (c. 520–505) signed at least six vases as painter and ten, later in his career and for other painters (mainly Onesimos), as potter. None of his surviving vases seems less than perfect, and this is not the result of any reluctance of scholars to look for his hand in lesser works. He likes big craters, especially the calyx crater, but decorated other shapes too, including cups for the potter Kachrylion. His own potting career may have started at the same time as his painting, despite the lack of signatures and the fact that two of his calyx craters were made by Euxitheos. It has been suggested that a new interest in neck amphorae with twisted handles is due to him. Certainly his treatment of two which have survived is special and looks forward to important styles of the early fifth century – one with black body and pictures only on the neck; the other with black neck and single figures on either side in the free black field without ground lines. This is a treatment copied by others and to be perfected by the Berlin Painter.

His style is 'classic' for the period, with few decided oddities. His heads are deep from front to back, with neat, calm features. Eyes tend to be narrow and the finely lashed ones tend to open towards the tear duct. Lip contours are generous, ears heavy-lobed with careful inner markings on larger heads. Hair contours are incised or reserved. The fingertips, often with nails marked, turn up sharply and the fingers are thin and brittle. On the body he likes to contour even minor areas, like the muscles beside the knee caps. Ankle bones are triangles with double front lines. He enjoys the texture of pattern, whether it be the black and white of patterned cloaks, Amazon dress and furnishing, or the thinned paint on lionskin or hair, when drawn in separate locks, or the cup on [25].

His masterpieces, the craters, display originality of theme and composition. On the Paris crater Herakles' fight with Antaios is a new creation [23]. The

Libyan giant should be lifted bodily to remove him from his strength-restoring mother Earth, but Euphronios wants to make the most of big figures on a big vase, contrasting Herakles' neat coiffure of relief ringlets and trim beard with the uncouth giant, eyes rolling, teeth bared, hair and beard wild (oddly like other representations of Libyans). The giant's right arm is already paralysed, his fingers limp. His leg doubled beneath him leaves us a glimpse of the sole of his foot, a view of which Euphronios seems fond. Notice his use of thinned paint for the giant's hair, in the furrows of his belly muscles, on the lionskin. The distraught women are at reduced scale more because they are less important and have to be upright on the shallow frieze than because the artist understood perspective.

The New York crater offers another first with winged Sleep and Death carrying from the Trojan battlefield the body of Sarpedon [*22, Frontispiece*]. The Berlin crater [*24*] gives us Euphronios' studies of posture rendered in line – successfully; but less so on another Paris crater, fragmentary, with somewhat awkwardly poised revellers tumbling over slippery wineskins. This sort of drawing can freeze the deliberate action of dance, fight or sport more plausibly than the unrehearsed upset.

There are other majestic treatments of myth – Herakles fighting Amazons on a volute crater [*29*], with Geryon on one cup [*26*], gods attending Peleus and Thetis on another. But everyday life had become no less inspiring a source for the Pioneers – witness the chastisement – for what, I wonder – on [*30*] (in Beazley's drawings) and the ladies' party on [*27*]. One girl here toasts Leagros, who is praised by Euphronios on a dozen other vases which probably belong to the decade 515–505. The grandest party of them all was on a crater, fragments of which are now in Munich [*25*], and here Smikros is named [*head details, left*].

SMIKROS [*31, 32*] (*c.* 510–500) signs two stamnoi and a twisty-handled amphora as painter, and on the former he praises the beauty of Antias: an affection for vase shapes and a boy which he shares with Euphronios among the Pioneers. Another stamnos, a psykter and two pelikai are attributed to him. If the associations of the name on vases refer to one man he seems to have been a playboy artist. Beazley called him an 'imitator of Euphronios'. Two points of comparison we have observed, and may add an interest in pattern and the free field single figures on the amphora. The differences, apart from some lack of enterprise in composition, are in the drawing which, though precise, skimps ears, has boneless awkward hands, dwells here and there on a head or body, then hurries over dress. His satyrs are his best creations, heavily moustached and bearded, balding, their noses less snub than broken.

EUTHYMIDES [*33–7*] is Euphronios' rival – but no doubt also friend – in the Pioneer Group: slightly junior in years, perhaps, but no imitator and his equal in invention and draughtsmanship, with a subtly different approach to his art. His friendly 'as never Euphronios' is inscribed beside a *tour de force* of linear anatomy [33.2] and his free, sometimes lavish use of thinned paint for anatomical detail lends his figure work a decidedly more sculptural air. He was free with inscriptions too, naming himself seven times, his father (Pollias the sculptor) thrice, with other mottoes and legends: an extrovert (compare their names – Euthymides 'good spirit', Euphronios 'good sense'!). choosy in his affections, naming Megakles as beautiful, but identifying many other contemporaries on his vases (including Leagros, Phayllos, Smikythos, Sosias).

His figures are heavier, meatier than Euphronios'. He usually incises the hair outline and avoids relief ringlets. In general he relies more on line than pattern. There are few lashed eyes, simpler ears with a centre tick or hook, the loose flesh of the scrotum is marked, the feet long and flat, fingers rubbery. The cloaks stand up in stiff folds at the back of the neck. In the florals there are fewer lotuses, their members separated. He seems to have preferred the large belly amphorae (Type A) for his work to craters, and the one volute crater from his hand confines figures to the neck, not body (contrast Euphronios [29]). The masterpieces are in Munich. On [33] Hector arms, watched by his parents. Parts of figures are often allowed to overlap the border (as on [34]) but here the upper border is less happily broken. Less than perfect, too, is the way Hector's profile head joins his frontal body, but on the back of the vase we have the proudly successful display of three-quarter front and back (we could have wished him similar success with the left leg of the dancer on the right). The leader of the revels is on the left, labelled 'komarchos'. On [34] a mildly protesting Helen is carried off by Theseus. Korone tries to drag her back (her name and Helen's were transposed accidentally by the artist) and Peirithoos looks round to the other side of the vase where an old man and two girls react appropriately to their ages and sex.

Euthymides' contribution to the group of twisty-handled amphorae with single figures has a satyr and a youth. With the wrestlers on a psykter [36] he makes his bid for a three-quarter leg but the frontal outline, displaced knee and profile foot fail him. Frontal faces had been saved for grotesques hitherto, and they still only succeed where distorted features are called for, as for the piper [35] (compare Euphronios' toper [25]).

34

Euthymides had his imitators too, and we shall return to them, but there are also masters whose work is related to his. PHINTIAS [38–42] (c. 525–510) might well be his senior, and we have already remarked his inscribed compliment to the younger man. He signs seven vases as painter (erratically – Phintias, Phitias, Philtias, Phintis) and three as potter (two are cockle-shell vases, the other a cup for a red figure artist of quality [49]). He is a more finicky artist than Euthymides, likes relief ringlets and details of nails, knuckles, soles of feet, and sometimes a ladder pattern along the breast bone. Like Psiax, he incises some inner muscle and dress lines, without painting them. Compared with Euthymides his figures are less plausible and alert, the dress too is stiffer and lacks the sweeping folds. He loves drawing vases and we have studies of a wide selection of shapes in symposia, fountain scenes and once in a vase shop.

A cup which he decorates for Deiniades has something of early Epiktetos [42]. Another signed cup is [39] with a fine centaur and puzzling assault. At this scale he is probably at his most effective. His more precious work appears on the big amphorae. On [41] Apollo and Artemis rescue their mother Leto from Tityos. He was a giant, and shown as such in black figure, but Phintias makes him smaller than the deities, who then have both divinity and stature on their side, and this weakens the narrative. But with an athlete on the other side of the vase he makes a good try at a three-quarter leg. The Tarquinia vase offers all the detailing of locks, side-burns, lashes and finger nails [40]. Phintias makes his mark better in heads and dress.

HYPSIS (c. 510) signs a hydria and leaves his name also on a kalpis [43, 44], the old and new versions of the water jar, both of which he shows on his kalpis [44], where girls draw water at the fountain of Dionysos ('krene Dionysia'). His figures have a degree of Euthymidean weight and are as well composed although somewhat less detailed. Best are his arming Amazons, a group skilfully set in the rectangular field, but he has not learned how to adjust the trumpeter's back to her left arm.

The DIKAIOS PAINTER [45–7] is another with Euthymidean associations, but he works in black figure too, in a competent fussy style approaching Psiax. He often uses black figure florals on his red figure vases, where the figures stand tight-lipped and expressionless in compositions which recall the duller black figure of the day, but with individual figures which seem straight copies of Euthymides. The drinking and wenching on a psykter and kalpis [46, 47] are more effectively portrayed and show some originality of pose. They are favourite shapes for these studies of contemporary life.

There are a few other individual pieces of merit which belong here. Phintias potted a cup for another, no less talented, artist to decorate [49]. Gorgos potted another [48], with a youth holding a hare within, in a style very like the Phintias cup, and a notable myth scene on one side which shows a fine sense of dramatic detail – Achilles fights Memnon whose spear has pierced Achilles' shield and so is ineffective, and whose mother Eos, distraught, has torn her dress and bared her bosom in dismay. A Sosias was mentioned on various Pioneer vases. The potter Sosias makes a fine cup [*50*] for a painter, the SOSIAS PAINTER, a late Pioneer (*c.* 510–500). The exterior presents an unusual massing of figures for this technique, with Herakles led into the full assembly of Olympus, bristling with details of attributes and dress. Under a handle is an outlined head of the Moon (?). Within, Achilles binds Patroklos' arm. Here the painter is absorbed with pattern – on armour, cap, the most trivial details of anatomy. Patroklos, squatting on his shield, bracing his left leg against the border, is an unusual and early study in distraction and pain. Both men are intent, wide-eyed, and the artist anticipates later, more accurate rendering of the eyes by opening them realistically, with the pupil forward. This shows what can happen when an artist momentarily abandons what he has been taught and looks around him. It also, for its rarity, shows how small a part still direct observation was playing.

The Sosias Painter used touches of white on the bandage and for Patroklos' bared teeth, and outside the cup he rendered in relief the pomegranates held by a goddess. Elsewhere we have seen the Pioneers use relief for ringlets or occasional florals, but they generally avoided colour and other relief aids. One vase, close in style and spirit to their work, has more of the experimental about it – the GOTHA CUP (*c.* 500) [*51*]. Within, the red figure lover and his lad are accompanied by a dog drawn in the Six technique – white paint on the black ground, with painted and incised details. Outside, the symposiasts are outline drawn on a white ground, with black handle palmettes. These are techniques which had been developed by black figure artists, and we might now consider whether the Pioneers ever practised the old technique. The Dikaios Painter we might regard almost as a convert from the old to the new, not trained originally in red figure. The only examples of what might be Pioneer black figure (or in related technique) appear where we might best expect them – on official work where the old technique was required or appropriate – Panathenaic vases and votive plaques for the Acropolis (and see below for work on white ground). The material is fragmentary and certainty impossible, but two plaques, decorated with outline figures, part incised, on a white ground, are worth a second look. One, with an Athena [*52*], was dedicated by Pollias, Euthymides' sculptor father, and in a style compatible with his son's works. The other [*53*], a larger slab, shows a storming warrior with a satyr shield blazon repeated by Euthymides, and inscribed 'Megakles kalos'. The Megakles has been erased and Glaukytes substituted, no doubt after the ostracism of Megakles in 486 BC: he is elsewhere praised by Euthymides and Phintias. Quite apart from their own possible black figure work, by challenge and example the Pioneers influenced an important series of all-black-figure vases of the last years of the century – the Leagros Group (*ABFH* pp. 110f.).

22 *Calyx crater signed by Euphronios. Sleep and Death carry Sarpedon. (See Frontispiece.)*
H. 45·8

23 *Calyx crater signed by Euphronios. Herakles and Antaios*

24.1–3 Calyx crater by Euphronios

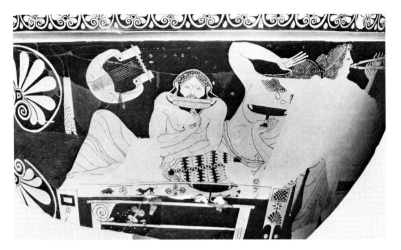

25 Calyx crater by
Euphronios

26.1, 2 Cup signed by
Euphronios. Outside –
Herakles and Geryon

27 *Psykter signed by Euphronios*

28 *Psykter by Euphronios. Death of Pentheus*

29 *Volute crater by Euphronios. Herakles and Amazons*

30.1, 2 *Neck pelike by Euphronios*

31 Neck amphora
by Smikros

32.1 Stamnos signed
by Smikros. H. 38·5

32.2 Detail of 32.1

33.1 Belly amphora (Type A) signed by Euthymides. Hector arms

33.2 Reverse of 33.1

34.1, 2 Belly amphora (Type A) by Euthymides. Theseus and Helen

35 *Kalpis by Euthymides*

37 *Neck amphora by Euthymides*

36 *Psykter signed by Euthymides*

38.1, 2 Hydria by Phintias. H. 51·5

39.1, 2 Cup signed by Phintias

40.1, 2 Belly amphora (Type A)
signed by Phintias. Apollo and
Herakles with tripod; and reverse

41.1 Belly amphora (Type A) by Phintias. Apollo, Artemis, Tityos and Leto

41.2 Reverse of 41.1

42 Cup signed by Phintias. Herakles and Alkyoneus

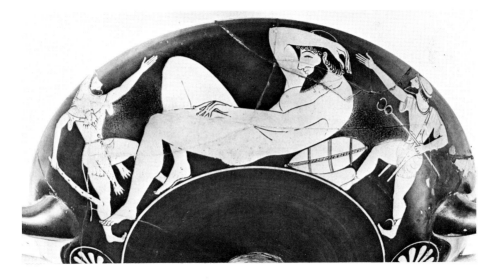

43 Hydria signed by Hypsis. Amazons

44 Kalpis signed by Hypsis

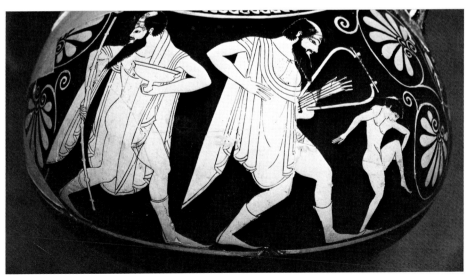

47 Psykter by the Dikaios Painter

48.1 Cup signed by Gorgos. Achilles and Memnon

48.2 Reverse of 48.1. W. 18

48.3 Interior of 48.1

49 Cup signed by Phintias as potter

50.1 *Cup by the Sosias Painter. Achilles and Patroklos*

50.2 *Outside of 50.1. Introduction of Herakles to Olympus*

51.1 Cup. White ground

51.2 Interior of 51.1

52 Votive plaque by Euthymides

53 Plaque by Euthymides. W. 52

Cup painters

At least eight out of ten of the red figure vases which survive from the first generation of practice in the new technique are cups. The Andokides Painter and the Pioneers had preferred the larger shapes, and on these, with their larger figure scenes, the new drawing skills could be most effectively displayed and developed. Many Pioneer cups are large and showy pieces – 'parade cups' (*Prachtschalen*) – a style with a brief following. For ordinary trade purposes the new red figure meant cups. These do not display the variety of forms met in the black figure Little Masters. The earliest red figure cups are of Type A – 'eye cups' for their characteristic decoration (although there are some without eyes and not all eyes are on Type A) – a shape invented for black figure perhaps by Exekias, and deriving its unbroken body profile and scheme of decoration with eyes from an earlier tradition in East Greece. The early red figure eye cups, as [66], have the same offset, tall feet as their black figure contemporaries (*ABFH* figs. *173*, *178*), looking like a flat pierced disc beneath (as in the Little Masters), but soon being fashioned with hollow, trumpet-like feet, painted black within.

The development of the scheme of decoration for red figure eye cups has been clearly defined by Beazley. It spans mainly the 520's and 510's, but the type is not then forgotten, it has a brief survival into Late Archaic (Colmar and Antiphon Painters) and the scheme was being used in black figure well into the fifth century. The earliest are mostly bilinguals with a black figure tondo inside the cup, usually a simple figure subject, and red figure outside. There are early all-red-figure cups too, and on all these the usual decoration is of single figures between the eyes, with palmettes by the handles. Later the palmettes and eyes may change places ('palmette-eye' cups, as [68]) destroying the mask-like effect, which disappears completely wherever the eyes are themselves replaced by animals, generally sphinxes or winged horses [93].

The palmettes on the bilinguals are almost always closed like enormous fans [61], but later the leaves separate and open, and while the heart of the palmette was at first often painted red it is now blacked in with a small reserved centre. The leaves are rarely given centre spines. A variety of lotuses or buds may be attached. The eyes themselves come to lose the boldly marked tear duct, square off at the inner corner, and tend to lose the white ring in the pupil.

The eye scheme appears in its later form also on cups of Type B, as [48], where the outline runs in a flowing curve down to a shallow step on the flaring trumpet foot, while within the cup, just below the lip, there is a sharp ridge.

On both these cup shapes, and with increasing frequency, eyes may be omitted altogether and the figures fill each side in long friezes, with or without handle palmettes, or the decoration may be confined to the interior, the outside left black. The quality of potting and gloss paint had improved in these years and the appeal of plain black areas was better appreciated and achieved. One other cup shape should be mentioned since it becomes increasingly popular – Type C. This has a concave lip, more abruptly offset than that of a black figure band cup, and the line of the bowl runs down the squat stem to a moulding on the flattish foot. Some have this foot and body but a straight lip. The general effect is heavier, more serviceable than the delicate stemmed cup. Type C's can be decorated outside as well as in, but often inside only, and are most popular all black.

The few cups painted by the Pioneers are of the frieze type, without eyes, giving fuller value to the figure composition. They are at any rate later than the main run of the eye cups and offer other variations in the cup pattern, such as the sword-like centre leaf to the palmettes on Phintias' cup, overlapping its tendril [39]. One or two of the specialist cup painters spent part of their time, and not always early in their careers, painting larger shapes (Oltos, Epiktetos), and there are lesser artists (or less prolific) whose work can readily be related to that of the Pioneers. But generally the cups called for a different idiom, less reliant on subtle intensities of detail, more on economical and telling line. They offered less room for the set mythological tableaux and their function at any rate encouraged depiction of Dionysiac or party scenes in which the new licence in graphic display of postures and action, novel in figurative art, was fully exploited. On the cups we can as readily measure the promise that the new technique held for the representation of action and emotion.

There are few technical peculiarities to be observed. The fine coral-red ground had been used for black figure first by Exekias, is similarly used outside red figure cups by Skythes, and appears on areas of some all-red-figure cups, usually filling the interior round the tondo, as [26], and on the zone below the figure scene outside (and above it if there is a Type C lip). It lent an extra richness to the colour texture of the vase, but was reserved for cups and a few other small vases in the Archaic period. Cup painters, like the painters of larger pots, used relief blobs for hair locks or relief details on florals and grapes, but only rarely on this smaller scale. Whole relief figures appear on a cup made for dedication on the Acropolis by the Euergides Painter [100] – men with horses, with details in red figure. There had been earlier East Greek cups decorated in this manner. Gilding is sometimes admitted on minor relief details of wreaths and the like.

OLTOS (c. 525–500) is probably the most interesting of the cup painters [54–65], for his range and long career and for his quality, which falls little short of the best in this class. He was a busy artist, known to have worked for at least six different potters including the cup specialist Kachrylion early in his career, Euxitheos (who also served Euphronios) rather later, and the Nikosthenes-Pamphaios workshop. He gives us his name on two cups made by Euxitheos but well over one hundred others can be attributed to him. His devotion to Memnon lasts through his career and the kalos inscriptions for him appear on nearly half his cups.

His earlier big vases are amphorae of the distinctive shape made in the Nikosthenes-Pamphaios workshop for the Etruscan market [56], and the stamnos showing Herakles fighting Acheloos, where he gives the monster a fishy rather than the usual bull's body, and is explicit about the breaking of its horn [54]. Pamphaios modelled budding horns by the handles of the vase to emphasise the theme. Later are other amphorae, one for Euxitheos, more Pioneer in style and pattern and of the new Type C shape. The psykter [58] is a cheerfully decorative vase of mummer dolphin-riders, each singing 'on a dolphin' ('epi delphinos'), who would appear sea-bound when the vase was set in a crater. The black figure tondos of Oltos' early cups [61] recall the Antimenes Painter. His red figure work on cups, except for set-pieces on some larger vessels, is characterised by a judicious economy of line in the anatomy, a long curving forehead-nose line with tight lips, down-curving to give an air

of smug cheerfulness. Feet are long and slim, ears a simple whorl. As on the Phintias cup, Oltos will sometimes fill his frieze with large reclining figures. In florals he favours distinctive lotus types, crowned with palmette leaves, or simpler, with plain ballooning centrepieces (on cups). Some palmette leaves are pointed or ribbed, and he has a few tondos of palmettes only (as did Psiax). On his larger cups for Euxitheos he puts a floral beneath the scenes [55], as did Euphronios. The one of which I show details gives a masterly and original rendering of the assembly of gods on Olympus with telling detail of gesture, glance and dress. Yet it is the brisk warrior and athlete figures of his eye cups in which his individuality is better appreciated. His other favourite subjects, apart from the Dionysiac and occasional bawdry, are heroic – Herakles, Theseus, Troy.

In many respects Oltos provides a link or element of continuity at a lower level between the styles of earliest red figure – Beazley thought he might have been a pupil of the Andokides Painter – and the Pioneers. Our next cup painter, EPIKTETOS [66–78, cover] (c. 520–490) has a similar background, since early in his career he painted a calyx crater for the potter Andokides, but he seems subsequently to have preferred specialising in the smaller vases, including plates [77, 78, cover] – a favourite Archaic shape which was being used by Paseas and Psiax as well as by other cup painters. He worked for several potters including Hischylos and the Nikosthenes-Pamphaios workshop, and is free with his signature – on nearly half the hundred or more vases surviving. A Hipparchos (probably not *the* Hipparchos – the vases seem too late, the man too old or dead) was his favourite boy. He signs one plate as both potter and painter (to dedicate on the Acropolis), so he was versatile, and he collaborated on one cup with the Euergides Painter.

His earliest cups are bilingual eye cups, as [66], but not as primitive as Oltos' first – none with red palmette hearts, no hesitancy in use of relief lines. He was a master of the circle – it is his tondos and plates we remember and he rather favoured cups decorated only within. The delicacy and accuracy of his line even in miniaturist work show how far yet how quickly progress in command of the brush had gone since the Andokides Painter's first attempts. His black figure shows a sureness and a discipline which few practitioners of the old technique could still muster [66]: his red figure an exquisite balance of line and detail, with restrained use of colour and pattern. Heads and limbs are more accurately proportioned than Oltos' and he will use the muted, paler paint where others dash on the relief line. His figures have that sculptural

plausibility which we see in the best early red figure and Beazley's much-quoted 'you cannot draw better you can only draw differently' does no less than justice to the greatest draughtsman of early red figure. But he was no sobersides. His myth scenes are few, and seldom highly original, but his depiction of the commonplace, of citizens at play, at bed or board (the same thing for Greeks, who reclined on beds for feasts), and his contribution to the development of the satyr as a psychological substitute study for man, plus a variety of new erotic imagery, represent a considerable advance on what black figure (we think of the Amasis Painter first) began to offer and set a significant new mood in the subject-matter of Greek art, no less important than the new narrative of the Pioneers.

His tondos are worth some attention – a favourite subject for the exercise of the aesthetics of geometry in composition. In black figure the primitive kneeling-running figure had served usefully for such fields. Now a subtler variety of kneeling, squatting, seated figures are used, action and object varied according to needs. Thus we see the same stooping, twisting figure used for a Minotaur [70], and two self-indulgers – a man with a chamber pot, a girl with dildos [71]. Cock-horse riders are commoner than cock riders in Greek art, and on the Castle Ashby plate [cover] he may have preferred to eliminate the monstrous in his study of fowl and boy.

The end of his career is enigmatic. He paints once for Python (a cup of the black figure Chalcidising shape [75]) who was potter for Douris, a Late Archaic artist, and is thought to have been affected by Douris' style; and once for Pistoxenos, a potter for Early Classical artists. I doubt whether he could have worked very much later than about 490, and his name will give us more trouble in the next chapter.

A few other cup painters, mainly early, can be placed here, their work in varying degrees related to Epiktetos. PHEIDIPPOS (c. 525–515) who may have worked exclusively for the potter Hischylos, paints eye cups, mainly bilingual, favouring plump little athletes with pigeon chests drawn in a sweeping curve and with tiny ears: pleasing, unambitious stuff [79, 80]. The THALIARCHOS PAINTER is recognised as the artist of the tops of some powder-box pyxides [81]. The BOWDOIN-EYE PAINTER gives somewhat sketchier but lively versions of the athlete [82], warrior and komast figures of the better early cup painters, while the SCHEURLEER PAINTER [84] renders them with less assurance about proportion and details. The DELOS PAINTER [83] has more of the linear skills of Oltos and Pheidippos and a particularly delicate black figure hand for tondos. And the WINCHESTER PAINTER redeems some poor draughtsmanship with wit [85]. Finally, the HISCHYLOS PAINTER, named for the potter who had also employed Epiktetos and Pheidippos, who offers a good example of a cup with a full palmette complex by the handles and intent, competent figures; still puzzled, though, with the proper foreshortening of a shield and drawing a profile plus partial-frontal view [86]. His hand is also seen on a larger vase of a new shape – the bell crater.

SKYTHES (c. 520–505), 'the Scythian', is a loner [88–91]. He signs four cups, has a score of others attributed to him and two standlets. His favourite boy is Epilykos. His bilinguals are not of the usual type, but red figure inside with black figure on a coral-red ground outside – three are known. Unlike the majority of Greek artists Skythes seems a comic by intention. Beazley is always quotable and will be cited often in this book: of Skythes – 'who purposely paints men worse than they are'. We might add that his gods are no better than his men – hero and villain may look equally brutish – as the Theseus punishing what might be intended for Skiron by his cliff [90]. He imparts a perky charm even to his animals, but it is in his expressively individual faces that his off-beat humour is caught, and his drawing, if not ambitious, is competent and canonical. If he was of foreign birth or background, but

59

Athenian training, his view of Athens' life and myth might have been different enough to show in his work. Scythians had become familiar in Athens some twenty years before. If his name is not a true indication of his descent it may at least be a sobriquet denoting a rather *outré* view of life. Two black figure plaques on the Acropolis are signed by a Skythes, almost certainly the same artist in a more reverent mood. Beazley wondered whether the PEDIEUS PAINTER was really Skythes in later years. Both praise Epilykos (who is, incidentally, an athlete on a Phintias vase) and the mood is the same [92], but the Pedieus Painter is rather more crude and tasteless.

Nikosthenes and his younger partner and successor Pamphaios made an important series of black figure vases, many in original shapes for Athens, mainly for the export market (*ABFH* pp. 64f.). Their red figure is less exciting, but Pamphaios made amphorae of the Nikosthenic type for Oltos [56], there are some big kantharoi and an odd spouted cup [98]. Both Oltos and Epiktetos worked for them but their regular red figure artist we know as the NIKOS-THENES PAINTER (not the same as the black figure 'N Painter'). He paints [93–8] standard eye cups, though not the very earliest, some 'palmette-eyes' and cups with friezes, the best, after which he was first named, being his London cup with Sleep and Death. There is also a red figure Nikosthenic pyxis [97]. The style is brisk and adequate, the figures rather heavy and sometimes ill-proportioned, filling space in a rather old-fashioned black figure manner, and clinging to black figure subsidiary ornament. Other products of the workshop, still busy until at least 510, earned their way with original but unsubtle themes [99], poorly but explicitly executed.

The EUERGIDES PAINTER [100–4] (c. 515–500) is named for the potter for whom he most often worked (he also painted for Chelis). He collaborated with Epiktetos on one cup, doing the exterior, and he shares Epiktetos' admiration of Hipparchos, but all there is of the older master in his work is the common range of themes. His best work seems to be on a cup he made for dedication on the Acropolis [101], showing Athena beside a vase painter, who is painting the interior of a cup, on a potter's wheel, and metalworkers. This looks like a deliberate dedication by the painter, or more probably by the potter, Euergides, who may have done some metalwork on the side. The artisan areas were close together in Athens, and both crafts called for skill with furnaces. We have noted his exceptional cup from the Acropolis with part-relief figures [100], and he may also be responsible for two remarkable hemicylindrical stands (copying an Etruscan shape, but not a demonstrably Nikosthenic model this time) carrying sphinxes [103] and a winged goddess with heads in the round and combining red figures, Six and outline techniques. These are, for this artist, *tours de force*. His other cups are not of the earliest – no eye cups (unless his early phase is as the Delos Painter, which Beazley considered) – and he is fond of animals besides the handles (winged horses, griffins, sphinxes). Execution here varies from what looks like rather unskilled copying to care-

60

less repetition of stock themes. His quality, as with many such second-rate though prolific artists, is given away by incompetence or lack of detail in features such as ears and hands or the body shown through dress, and some odd proportions like shallow heads. The EPELEIOS PAINTER [105, 106] apes Epiktetos in a similar way, indeed some of his cups look like rough copies of the master. The style generally is far weaker than the Euergides Painter's and he may be an older man since he paints some eye cups with fan palmettes. On [106] his satyr Terpon finds 'the wine is sweet' ('hedus hoinos').

Several cups in the manner of the Euergides Painter, and one or two by him, carry rather unusual single-word inscriptions. One is 'paidikos', which in the context of vase painting must mean 'boyish' rather than 'childish': the other is 'prosagoreuo' – 'I greet [you]'. They appear also on a number of alabastra in closely related style. On one of these 'paidikos' is written with 'epoiesen', as though it were the potter's name, but more likely his nickname. In this GROUP OF THE PAIDIKOS ALABASTRA (c. 520–500) the best vases are white ground and are signed by the potter Pasiades. He was not the painter too since he signs another vase as painter (a white ground lekythos). This PASIADES PAINTER was a cut above the Euergides Painter, to whom he is otherwise closely related (also in admiration of Hipparchos) and these are charming, slight vases where the prettiness of Archaic detail is not overpowered by a black ground. The rest of the Group, mainly red figure, is coarser. The scene on the alabastron [107] is 'rolled out' in the photograph.

It has not been easy in this survey of cup painters to discern major painter-potter groups. Painters were sometimes footloose, some potteries may have been large establishments, and at any rate potter signatures are still few and potter attribution by shape not as well developed a study as painter attribution. So there are no neat divisions and we are grateful where painter, potter and kalos signatures repeat often enough, with some congruence of style and theme, to reveal at least a temporary trend in the potters' quarter. A few other potters deserve special mention, and their employment of painters. Hermaios signed four cups as potter and his HERMAIOS PAINTER [108–10] also worked, probably later, for the potter Kachrylion. He is a good painter with rather heavy-headed sleepy-looking figures of Oltan physique, using devices like double edges to chiton tops, recalling painters of larger pots, even the Pioneers. Kachrylion also employed Oltos and he made Euphronios' two great cups. He must have been an influential figure to command such quality.

Chelis was another important potter working about 515–500, and although few signatures survive his painters are known to have included Oltos and the Euergides Painter. Two of his signatures appear on cups by the CHELIS PAINTER [111], on one of which part of the painting is by Oltos. The THALIA PAINTER also worked for both Chelis and Kachrylion, but started his career earlier. He is at times a good artist, best on a cup in Berlin [112] whose interior offers studies of self-love by boy and girl, and love-making helped out by a slipper (wielded by the girl). This is executed with the greatest care, using relief hair locks and tackling difficult postures with near success.

There remain to be named a few other painters, mainly of the last decade of the sixth century, who work still in the tradition of the early cups rather than with the new freedom and mood of some contemporary artists whom we have to consider in the next chapter. Beazley was not sure whether the EPIDROMOS PAINTER ([113, 114]: named from an often repeated kalos name) was the early phase of APOLLODOROS [116–18] who leaves his name on two cups. It seems probable, to judge from the distinctive features with small, deep-set eyes, long nose lines and, for example, some George Bernard Shaw style beards. Some figures look mannered in proportions or pose [116]. Some of the early cups have a spaced double line round the tondo, which is not otherwise an early feature. The ELPINIKOS PAINTER is another candidate for identity with Apollodoros and has an original way with tondos – the Theseus-Sinis Group [115] and a profile head of the Moon on an unpainted disc.

The AMBROSIOS PAINTER ('if bad he is never dull' – Beazley) might be excused his summary draughtsmanship for the sheer verve of his figures, not without some skill in posture and composition. I show his more sober works – a boy fishing, with lobster-pot and a shy octopus, and myth [119–21]. The PAINTER OF THE AGORA CHAIRIAS CUPS shows a devotion to buxom girls [122] and a skill at drawing them which is distinctive and uncommon for this period. Others are less readily characterised but have some pleasing passages and themes: the KISS PAINTER [123], the CARPENTER PAINTER [124], the SALTING PAINTER [125]. The HEGESIBOULOS PAINTER is a comedian like Skythes, named for the potter of the New York cup with the weary old Hebrew gentleman and his dog [126].

A few of these painters have been second rate. Of the third rate, Beazley's 'Coarser Wing', we have promoted the Nikosthenes-Pamphaios workshop, as seems deserved, and mentioned the many Epeleian cups after the Euergides Painter. Of others little need be said, less illustrated [127, 128]. They copy their betters, generally following the Epiktetan range of subjects, repeating stock themes of satyrs and youths with pots or wineskins, or single warrior figures. The PITHOS PAINTER and others reach a degree of abstraction with these on Type C cups decorated inside only, that has almost an appeal of its own after the discipline of most work in these years [128]. But the proportion of red figure work of this quality is far lower than that of black figure.

Aspects of the Pottery Trade

The significance of the 'epoiesen' ('made') and 'egrapsen' ('painted') inscriptions on vases for determining names of potters or owners and painters has been discussed in *ABFH* pp. 11f., and some features of the inscriptions peculiar to red figure will be mentioned later. For this and the succeeding

54 Stamnos by Oltos. Herakles and Acheloos. H. 27·5

55. 1–3 Cup signed by Oltos. Zeus;
Aphrodite; Athena

56 *Nikosthenic amphora by Oltos. Chiron with the child Achilles. H. 37*

57.1, 2 *Belly amphora (Type C) by Oltos. Briseis and Achilles. H. 40*

58.1, 2 Psykter by
Oltos. H. 30·2

59 Cup by Oltos. Poseidon

60 Cup by Oltos

61.1 Cup by Oltos.
Nereid. W. 32

61.2 Interior of 61.1.
Hermes

62 Cup by Oltos.
Peleus and Atalanta

63 Cup by Oltos

64 Cup by Oltos

*65 Cup by Oltos.
Herakles fights Kyknos*

66.1, 2 *Cup signed by Epiktetos H. 13·5*

67.1, 2 *Cup signed by Epiktetos*

68 *Cup signed by Epiktetos*

69 *Cup signed by Epiktetos*

70 *Cup by Epiktetos. Minotaur. W. 11*

71 *Cup by Epiktetos*

72 Cup by Epiktetos.
Herakles and centaurs

74 Cup by Epiktetos

73 Cup by Epiktetos

*75.1 Chalcidising cup
signed by Epiktetos.
Herakles and Busiris*

75.2 Interior of 75.1

*76 Cup–skyphos by
Epiktetos. H. 9·5*

77 Plate signed by
Epiktetos. W. 19·4

78 Plate signed by
Epiktetos. W. 18·7

79 Cup by Pheidippos

80 Cup by Pheidippos

81 Pyxis lid by the Thaliarchos Painter. W. 4

82 Cup by the Bowdoin Eye Painter (name vase)

83 Cup by the Delos Painter

84 Cup by the Scheurleer Painter

85.1, 2 Cup by the
Winchester Painter
(name vase)

86 *Cup by the Hischylos Painter*

88 *Cup by Skythes. Hermes*

87 *Bell crater fr. by the Hischylos Painter. H. 17*

89 *Cup signed by Skythes.*
Herakles and Eurystheus

90.1, 2 *Cup signed by Skythes.*
Theseus and Skiron

91 *Cup by Skythes*

92 *Cup by the Pedieus Painter*

93.1, 2 Cup by the Nikosthenes Painter. W. 32·5

94 Cup by the Nikosthenes Painter. Athena's chariot;
Herakles, Apollo and the tripod

95 *Cup by the Nikothenes Painter. Herakles and Alkyoneus*

96 *Cup by the Nikosthenes Painter. Hermes and cattle*

97 *Nikosthenic pyxis by the Nikosthenes Painter*

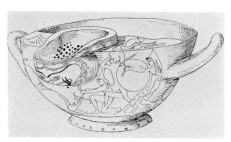

98 *Spouted cup by the Nikosthenes Painter. H. 12*

99.1, 2 Kantharos signed by
Nikosthenes as potter

100 Cup fr. with relief figure
by the Euergides Painter (?)

101 Cup by the Euergides Painter. Potter and metalworker

102 Cup by the Euergides Painter

103 Stand by the Euergides Painter (?). H. 26·2

104 Cup by the Euergides Painter.
Herakles and the Lion

105 Cup by the Epeleios Painter

106 Cup by the Epeleios Painter

107 Alabastron by the Pasiades Painter.
White ground

108 *Cup by the Hermaios Painter*

109 *Cup by the Hermaios Painter*

110 *Cup by the Hermaios Painter. Dionysos*

111 *Cup by the Chelis Painter*

112 *Cup by the Thalia Painter*

113 *Cup by the Epidromos Painter*

114 *Cup by the Epidromos Painter*

115 *Cup by the Elpinikos Painter. Theseus and Sinis*

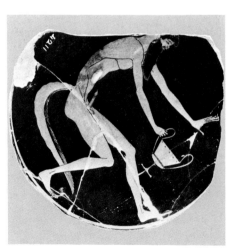

116 *Cup by Apollodoros*

117 *Cup by Apollodoros*

118 *Cup by Apollodoros. Theseus and Minotaur*

119 *Cup by the Ambrosios Painter*

120 *Cup by the Ambrosios Painter. Hephaistos*

121 *Cup by the Ambrosios Painter. Nessos and Deianira. W. 9·9*

122 *Cup by the Painter of the Agora Chairias cups*

123 *Cup by the Kiss Painter (name vase)*

124 *Cup by the Carpenter Painter (name vase)*

125 *Cup by the Salting Painter*

126 *Cup by the Hegesiboulos Painter. Coral red around tondo*

127 *Cup by the Poseidon Painter. Pyrrhic dance*   128 *Cup by the Pithos Painter. Youth at symposion*

period these have been supplemented by a detailed study of the potter work of the signed and unsigned vases, a field in which Professor Bloesch has been prominent, but it cannot be said as yet to have made a profound difference to our view of life in the potters' quarter. It is clear enough, now that painters' signatures are more common, that painters could and often did move from one potter to another, so an account based on potter traditions might not run in step with one based on painter traditions. Signatures of any sort remain rare, but we may observe that some 30 per cent of Early Archaic vases with painter signatures also carry potter signatures, while only 15 per cent of potter-signed vases are signed also by painters (22 per cent, ignoring Nikosthenes and Pamphaios: barely two hundred signatures in all are involved).

While several potters employed both black figure and red figure artists, or, like Andokides, moved from black figure into red figure, it is notable that the best potters from about 520 on specialised in red figure or black figure, not both. Another element of specialisation, already noted, is the dominance of the cup shape for red figure work. This meant that most full dinner services were bound to be largely or partly black figure (except on Pioneer-stocked tables) until about 500 when a greater proportion of larger shapes began to be decorated in the new technique. The reason for this specialisation is not quite clear. It might have been, for instance, a matter of different proportional demand from the overseas market, especially Etruria, which remains our most important source for complete early red figure vases. Certainly, outside Athens, early red figure was particularly welcome in Etruria, which at any rate tended to attract only the better vases. Other markets, for the Greeks in South Italy, in Greece itself, and probably even in Athens, apart from those supplying dedications for major sanctuaries, were more conservative in their tastes, and continued even into the fifth century to handle more of the cheaper black figure vases. Since the potters' quarter was by this time well aware of the value of the Etruscan market, and had designed special lines for it, this may be responsible in some degree for the plethora of red figure cups. The Pioneer vases which attest in their inscriptions the close relationship between the artists of the Group and Athenian society, also went mainly to Etruria, where the point of the inscriptions must have been lost, together with the topical value of the kalos names, praising current beauties. It has been suggested that many sets of vases were ordered for particular feasts, where they were admired, then disposed of through a secondhand market to Etruria. This gives more point to the kalos names and topical allusions, but possibly the vases were long on public display in the potters' quarter before sale or choice for shipment, and it is often a painter who shows allegiance to a particular youth in his kalos inscriptions, where we would expect more diversity if different patrons were putting orders. And if the kalos were the patron, we would expect longer-lived kalos names.

Chapter Three

THE LATE ARCHAIC PAINTERS

The first generation of red figure artists explored almost all the new technique could offer. What follows generally involves a simplification of technique, except for the developing use of white ground for certain vases, and is otherwise expressed by more realistic draughtsmanship in terms of both detail and pose, and a growing realisation of how objects in the round can be depicted in a purely linear style. This is accompanied by a significantly new range of figure scenes which represent much more of a break with the black figure tradition, and a growing market for Athenian red figure both within Greece and in the West.

The use of colour and pattern on dress, inherited from black figure, now dies out, although there is occasional gilding and relief detail, as for relief ringlets in hair. The relief line remains important, both for outlines and for its use in contrast with thinner paint on dress or anatomy, but the better painters are more selective in its use for outline while the lesser use for the figure drawing a weaker mix which produces good black lines but lacks the body and crispness of the true relief line. The falling off in attention to minor details of anatomy (ears, eyelashes, knee caps, etc.), which helped identify the work of individual Pioneers, is replaced by a deeper interest in the pose and composition of the whole figures.

Foreshortening is still mainly confined to the treatment of objects (shields), torsos and very rarely now of heads in three-quarter view (generally with little success in this case). There are some good foreshortened views of feet, to be distinguished from the simple head-on views, but whole limbs are still given their full extent and only a shift in muscle line or knee cap suggests anything other than profile or frontal views. Thinned paint is sometimes used to indicate shading, as on shields [268], but the effect is not properly understood. The finest dress is rendered in multiple stacks of folds with neat zigzag hemlines, but in general the patterns are less angular, except in the hands of the unimaginative. Close-set lines often cover chitons, and done in black paint not thinned. Sometimes they help express the body forms, but ineptly, by running to the tip of a breast instead of contouring it. On broader areas of cloaks lines begin to break into long arcs, and eventually hooks or 'ticks' to suggest the broken hanging curves. During this period eyes open properly

89

with the pupils pushed to the front, and rounder goggle eyes are reserved by many painters for the ferocity, mock or real, of satyrs and Herakles.

Subsidiary decoration changes in character and importance. Black patterns are rarer now – all is red figure. There is a small range of floral bands for the larger vases and occasional elaborate cups – circumscribed palmettes, upright or on their sides, or set obliquely in pairs. Some painters keep handle palmette complexes on cups (as Douris). Some still attach exotic lotuses. Cup tondos are bordered again now, with maeander and square patterns which appear also as ground lines or borders on larger vases and lekythoi. These details often carry valuable clues to the identity of painters or workshops.

In the first quarter of the fifth century red figure production must roughly have doubled after its slow and specialist start. The full range of pottery shapes is now decorated in the technique. There are no important new shapes, simply refinements of old ones, such as the neat small Nolan neck amphorae, or changes in proportions. Painters certainly specialise more and the pot painters and cup painters are distinct although not totally exclusive groups. The divisions must depend more upon the potters employing them, where similar specialisation is apparent. Loyalty of painter to potter is by no means absolute, especially in early careers, but there are some stable teams – Douris with Python, Makron with Hieron, Brygos and his painter. If anything, most artists, especially potters, are less free with their signatures, yet there are suspected ancient forgeries of signatures (Epiktetos, Douris).

In the subject-matter of the scenes on the vases the most conspicuous change is in the number and variety of genre scenes, by no means confined to the symposion and palaistra. The myth scenes show far greater diversity. Many stock scenes are abandoned and replaced not by new conventions but by original compositions which generally have a short vogue within a workshop or are peculiar to single painters whose own interests – for instance the Kleophrades Painter and Troy – are more readily now perceived.

In these years Athens was settling to its new constitution devised by Kleisthenes after the tyranny of Peisistratos and his sons had been overthrown. This change, from tyranny to near democracy, is marked in art probably only in some change of myth symbolism (see Chapter Eight). In 490 the Persians were defeated at Marathon and the immense popularity of Nike (Victory) on Athenian vases from this time on is surely not unconnected. In 480 and 479 Persians occupied and sacked Athens. In itself, this seems to have done no more, perhaps, than oblige the potters, like other craftsmen and citizens, to rebuild, although we may detect a myth-born comment by a more sensitive artist, like the Kleophrades Painter again. There are other changes or novelties in subject-matter, belonging rather to the next period and only indirectly affected by the Persian Wars, being rather reflective of Athens' new mood of Empire. These were hectic and exciting years for the vase painters and it is sad that we are denied more than glimpses of what new ground was being broken

90

by their sculptor contemporaries. This is Archaic art full-blown. What follows is nostalgia and the more sober novelty of Classicism.

The Kleophrades Painter and the Berlin Painter

These are the two great pot painters of the early fifth century, arguably the two greatest red figure artists whose works and careers we can judge. Their achievements and very different qualities are probably best appreciated when they are 'compared and contrasted', in the terms of an examination paper. Beazley, who devoted several monographs and articles to them, made some telling comparisons – of the Kleophrades Painter: 'He may be said to play a kind of Florentine to the Berlin Painter's Sienese'; of the two: 'The painter of grace [Berlin Painter] and the painter of power.' Carry the comparison beyond terms of draughtsmanship or mood, to consideration of subject, periods of maximum activity and influence, and the contrast of intellectual force as well as artistry becomes the stronger. So we shall consider them together first, then their separate careers.

Both artists were trained in the Pioneer School of the late sixth century – it could hardly be otherwise – and owe more to the authority of Euthymides and Phintias than to the more academic and probably senior Euphronios. The Kleophrades Painter remains closer to the Pioneers in both style and mood, his figures are heavy with power, Archaic still both in the static compositions of arming and the palaistra, and in the vigour of battle or dance. The Berlin Painter's figures are lighter, more exquisitely drawn, with a subtler and subdued use of relief line for contour, concentrating on the individual or exploiting a special skill in combining two figures in one contour, rather than fuller compositions. The Kleophrades Painter seems closer to the Pioneers too in the main period of his activity and preference for the large craters which they favoured, while the Berlin Painter has a slightly different interest in crater shapes (including the bell and column crater) and a much greater one in smaller vases, especially amphorae, on which most of his later painting is seen. Comparing their careers in terms of shape popularity the overlap is not total and can only in part be explained by the Kleophrades Painter's (or his employers') conservative viewpoint.

In choice of subject both start, and to some degree maintain, a concern with the traditional Dionysiac, komos or athlete scenes, with the Berlin Painter devoting more of his later work to trivial genre occasions. Yet even in the Dionysiac scenes there is a contrast, the Kleophrades Painter's satyrs are lusty and intent, while the Berlin Painter's rarely raise more than an eyebrow, and in other myth the difference is yet more marked. The Berlin Painter is no innovator. He goes for the Olympians and, in a true blue way, for the Attic favourites – Athena and Herakles, Demeter and Triptolemos, Nike, together with a fair range of stock myth scenes to which he contributes delicacy of figure study rather than originality of narrative. The Kleophrades Painter's stock scenes are close to the Pioneer repertory, but he adds a series of original studies of Trojan scenes, mainly from the Iliad, which seem to fulfil what Exekias had promised in sympathetic understanding of how myth can serve as the mirror to life. Where the Berlin Painter is introspective in a special way, allowing us to share his pleasure in perfect line or isolated mood, the Kleophrades Painter invites us to reflect with him on the dilemmas of man and hero as does no other Greek vase painter: a robust intellectual, a poet of the stage rather than the drawing-room – and many would agree that we come nowhere closer to the quality of Classical Greece than in its stage poetry, with its humour, pathos, exploration of humanity through myth, a tradition beginning with the Homeric poems, which inspired both our artist and his contemporary, Aeschylus. The statuesque strength of his figures has led some scholars to believe that he was a Peloponnesian, perhaps a Corinthian, by training, but his early work in Athens is purely Pioneer, and if he later gives promise of what Early Classical sculpture in the Peloponnese will achieve, this may mean no more than that he reflects the birth of a new style, which Athenian sculptors were seldom to practise, and their vase painters therefore never to develop as the artists of the Peloponnese could. But this is part of another story, and we may turn now to separate consideration of the two masters' careers.

The Kleophrades Painter [129–42] is named after the potter whose signature appears on one of his two Paris cups, which are among the largest cups we know, some 50 cm. wide. The fashion for these exceptionally large vessels was started by the Pioneers with their 'parade cups'. They are quite impractical, especially with their shallow bowls, and they seem to have been intended simply as fields for fine drawing, and were therefore found appropriate for the export market and for dedication in sanctuaries at home. The signature of the potter, which appears also on at least two other vases (including cups for the painter Douris) names Kleophrades' father, Amasis, surely the famous black figure potter/painter. This is an important identification of a family in the profession. The Kleophrades Painter's own name is not known. He was for long described by scholars as 'Epiktetos II' because this signature appeared twice on an undistinguished pelike [142], and was so recorded in the first printing of this book; but the writer has subsequently been able to prove that the signatures are modern forgeries, and so the painter returns to anonymity. He seems at any rate to have been a reticent artist, learning his letters late, it may be, since there is some nonsense on his early works, naming no pretty youths, but writing kalos or kalos ei ('you are handsome') anonymously. His citharode reciting epic – the words 'as once in Tiryns . . .' issue from his mouth – is exceptional [138].

His painting career begins by 505, ends soon after 475, and over one hundred vases have been attributed to him. The vase shapes he decorates are as those of the Pioneers, later turning more to pelikai, stamnoi and kalpides. His early work can readily be mistaken for that of his master, Euthymides, especially the Type A amphorae with their black pattern borders [129], the famous pointed amphora in Munich [132], and another recently acquired in Berlin. One of his volute craters is unique in having two friezes on its neck. His best work comes after 500, with the Paris cups [*head details, left*] celebrating Herakles and Theseus and several calyx craters but there are masterpieces still in the 480's and later (and see the Boot Painter). His red figure pattern work is restricted, mainly upright palmettes, alternate ones enclosed, or oblique palmettes paired, with very rare lotuses. Of border or ground line patterns he likes the simple key or maeander, interrupted rather than broken (as by the Berlin Painter) by a box or cross in squares, and has other favourite maeander forms – crossing or composed of T's [132, 133]. He had learnt to paint black figure too and uses the technique for subsidiary friezes on some of his early amphorae and on a later loutrophoros [141], a ritual shape, where the old technique was appropriate. He also decorated in black figure some Panathenaic amphorae, some standard late sixth-century neck amphorae and perhaps a funerary plaque. A late cup has a figure frieze round the tondo, an elaboration met occasionally in the work of other painters (as Douris) as it had been in black figure.

His figure drawing has some distinctive features, especially in comparison with the Berlin Painter. He continues incising hair contours long after most other painters had stopped, but not obsessively. The ears on early figures have a strong forward projection (lobe and tragus) simplified later to a tighter circle. Eyes soon open at the inner corner with the pupils well forward, and often painted as a brown – not black – circle and dot. Nostrils often have a full S curve and lips may be outlined lending a somewhat disdainful expression. The deep recurved hook of the Pioneer collar bones gives place to straight lines, on smaller figures sometimes with a distinctive semicircle dip at the join. Nipples are ignored, the line from navel to pubis is usually black, not brown. Ankles are simple hooks, and although he shrinks from foreshortenings except of stomach patterns or shields, he observes well any relaxed stance. The stolidity of his figures does not render them immobile although it is more the exquisite detail of the Dionysiac revel on [132] which appeals than any light-footedness on the part of the mainly over-dressed participants. Here, though, he shows his cleverness with use of thinned paint and brushwork on hair and dress.

He prefers Dionysiac and komos subjects early, genre and athletic later, with a fondness for outfacing ('chalice') compositions. Stock myth scenes are from the Pioneer repertory, including an interest in Theseus and Herakles, but his special achievement is his handling of Trojan scenes. His treatment of the standard scenes is always novel, but some may be his own invention – the rescue of Aithra, mourning Achilles – and others may be unique. The last include the dramatic exchange of gifts between Ajax and Hector, and possibly the exchange between Glaukos and Diomedes. On the great Vivenzio (its first owner) hydria [135], the Sack of Troy is depicted as never before or since: not merely the cruelty – sacrilege, murder, rape, despair – but courage too, the Trojan woman fighting back with her pestle (the only courageous acts here are by Trojans); and liberation, old Aithra bemused at rescue by her grand-sons; and hope, Aeneas' escape with his son and father: the last two scenes turning away from the horrors between, the whole a comment on the emotion and excesses involved in the sack of a great city. In 480 and the year following, the Athenians had left their homes and looked back from Salamis to see their city burned by the Persians. This vase may represent not the first, and not the last occasion on which the Sack of Troy served as a paradigm for the horrors of war: a savage act of victory and vengeance, inflicted by Greeks, even if only in myth history, but of which no Greek, from Homer on, seemed particularly proud, and to which they repeatedly returned, as we might to the destruction of a Dresden, Coventry or Hiroshima. No other Greek vase painter approaches this: the muralists could hardly have done it better.

The Berlin Painter [143–61, 383] is now credited with nearly three hundred vases, most of which (Beazley's 'early') belong to the years from about 500 to about 480. The beginning of his career presents problems to which we can return, and there are traits in his painting which have led scholars to suspect him of deliberate Archaising, but his later work is decidedly duller, mainly on Nolan amphorae and lekythoi, running into the 460's. Of these later works [158, 160] Beazley wondered whether many were not imitation or school pieces, but they are not hesitant works, even if the charm is lost, and who copies a master's declining style? He is extremely reticent with kalos names and no potters' signatures have been found on what is certainly his work. His favourite scheme of decoration – single figures on either side of the vase, even where the action continues (Perseus and Gorgon, Zeus and Ganymede, Herakles and Apollo: [153, 150, 145]) – with notable reduction of subsidiary ornament, is reflected by the shapes he favours. These are amphorae: rarely belly amphorae, although his finest work appears here on Type A's [144, 146] and a Type C [152]; commonly neck amphorae [148, 149], especially the smaller ones including the later Nolans [160], and the early amphorae of Panathenaic shape [145, 151, 153] which are comparatively rare otherwise. His craters are often decorated in this austere manner, including some volute craters whose bodies are otherwise usually left black, but the fine [154] has a fuller group. The new popularity for the bell [150] and column craters begins here, and an interest in stamnoi, including one or two of odd, tall-necked form. Pelikai he paints [143] and hydriai, kalpides, even lekythoi and slim oinochoai, rather surprisingly, but they too can lend themselves to single-figure studies. His fuller compositions appear on craters, stamnoi, a dinos and, unusually, on a neck amphora with a busy Amazonomachy [149].

His florals vary little, with neat circumscribed palmettes which are black in the old manner, on his earliest work, and lotuses whose angular centrepieces come to divide into trefoil palmettes with elongating centre leaves. (These florals appear on otherwise black vases, the Group of the Floral Nolans, from his school, the Eucharides and Dutuit Painters.) His maeander border and ground patterns, however, are distinctive, with the maeander chopped into units, often paired, and totally interrupted by boxed X's (saltire crosses) or

chequer. Few contemporaries copy this, and rarely. His technique is impeccable – 'the lines are thin, equable, and flowing, not dry like Douris', nor wet, thick, and strong, like Kleophrades'' (Beazley). Hair lines are reserved, relief line contour used sparingly on faces, but we see the relief hair ringlets and detailing of eyelashes on the more elaborate works, as [146]. There are no exclusive tricks of anatomy, but a preference for dot rosette nipples, genitals askew on frontals, triangles in the linear patterns on chests, hips and stomachs, blond boys (Apollo, Ganymede [150]). Whole limbs are still not foreshortened but feet are well managed in three-quarter view from front or back, and a realistic disposition of belly pattern either side of the median on twisting torsos. Dot in circle earrings are worn by the women, and there are few vagaries in dress. We see long wavy lines in brown, or alternating sweeps, from left and right, on cloaks. On full dress there is a steady change from Archaic stacked folds to all-over verticals or Early Classical groups of verticals with a level, if wavy, hemline. In his later work the dress in particular shows that the ageing Berlin Painter was not immune to those symptoms of decaying

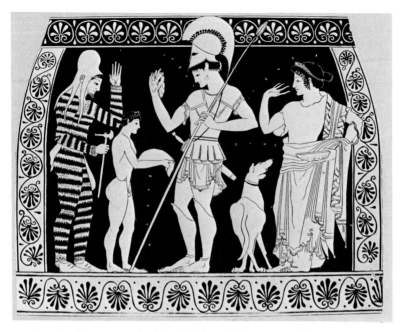

129.1 Belly amphora (Type A) by the Kleophrades Painter. Departure with extispicy

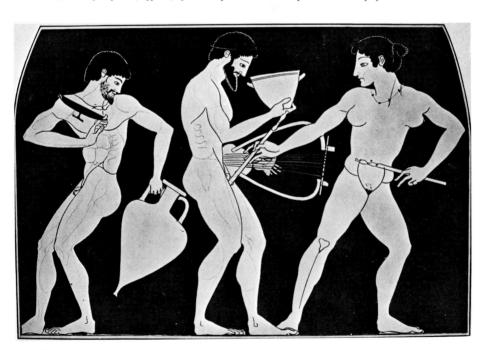

129.2 Reverse of 129.1

130 Calyx crater by the Kleophrades Painter. Return of Hephaistos. H. 43·8

131.1, 2 Calyx crater frs. by the Kleophrades Painter

132.1 Pointed amphora by the Kleophrades Painter. H. 56

132.2 Detail of reverse of 132.1

133 Calyx crater by the Kleophrades Painter

134 Volute crater by the Kleophrades Painter. Psychostasia

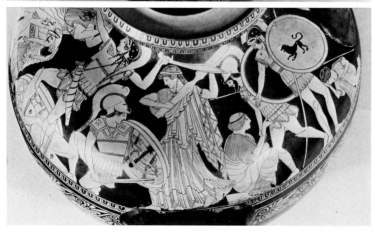

135 *Kalpis by the Kleophrades Painter. Aeneas and Anchises; Ajax and Kassandra; Death of
Priam; Andromache (?); rescue of Aithra*

136 Kalpis by the Kleophrades Painter

137 Stamnos by the Kleophrades Painter.
Theseus and Procrustes

138 Neck amphora by the Kleophrades
Painter. Rhapsode. H. 47

139 Skyphos fr. by the Kleophrades Painter.
Iris and centaurs

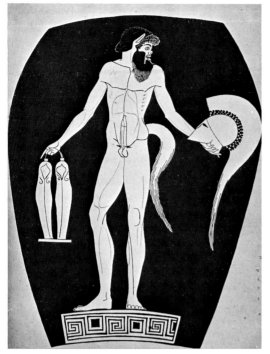

140 Neck amphora by the Kleophrades Painter

141 Loutrophoros amphora by the Kleophrades Painter. Prothesis. H. 81

142 Pelike by the Kleophrades Painter. H. 32.

143 *Pelike by the Berlin Painter (?). Death of Aigisthos*

145 *Panathenaic amphora by the Berlin Painter. Herakles*

144 *Belly amphora (Type A) by the Berlin Painter*

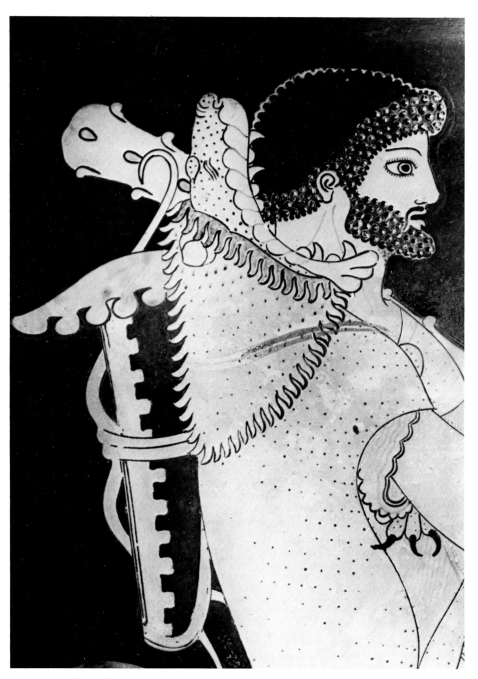

146.1 Reverse of 146.2. Herakles

146.2 Belly amphora (Type A) by the Berlin Painter. Athena. H. 79

147 *Kalpis by the Berlin Painter. Europa*

148 *Neck amphora by the Berlin Painter*

149 *Neck amphora by the Berlin Painter. Herakles and Amazons*

150 *Bell crater by the Berlin Painter. Ganymede. H. 33*

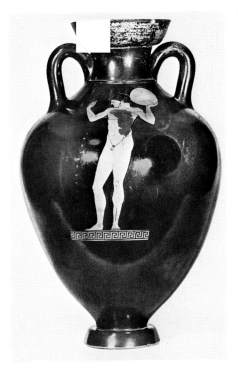

151 Panathenaic amphora by the Berlin Painter.
H. 48·5

152.1 Belly amphora (Type C) by the Berlin Painter.
Trainer. H. 42

153 Panathenaic amphora by the Berlin Painter.
Gorgon

152.2 Reverse of 152.1. Kitharode

154 *Volute crater by the Berlin Painter. Demeter and Triptolemos*

155 *Stamnos by the Berlin Painter. Infant Herakles and snakes*

156 *Hydria by the Berlin Painter. Herakles and Nereus*

158 *Neck amphora by the Berlin Painter. Helen and Menelaos*

157 *Hydria by the Berlin Painter. Apollo. H. 52*

159 Lekythos by the Berlin Painter. Nike

160 Nolan amphora by the Berlin Painter. Athena

161 Oinochoe by the Berlin Painter. Nike and youth

Archaism which are termed 'Mannerist' and which are considered in the next chapter.

His choice of subjects requires little further comment. Where action is required the figures are sure, elegant, and only on the earliest, near-Pioneer vases (if his), passionate [143]. His sympathetic treatment of animal studies, not conspicuous elsewhere in red figure except for the favoured horse, is worth observing [383]. The single figures or paired figures are the most telling. His most memorable works are his name vase in Berlin [144] where, boldly for red figure, he combines three figures in one contour – Hermes hastening past with cup and jug, a satyr (Oreimachos) with a lyre turning away, a fawn starting to the noise and movement around him; and a more recently revealed amphora in Basel [146] with a magnificently accoutred Athena on one side raising her jug for her favourite Herakles on the other, in his Number Ones, even the lionskin tail buttoned up.

A possibility which would revise our view of his early career and potential must be briefly discussed. Miss Talcott suggested that the cup signed by Gorgos [48] was early work of the Berlin Painter, and Martin Robertson elaborated the argument, adding the fine cup potted by Phintias [49], and pointing out how appropriate it would be if Gorgos were painter too in the light of the invariable gorgoneion shield devices which appear on black figure Panathenaic amphorae attributed (with a hesitation I share) to the Berlin Painter and his other fine red figure Gorgons. Beazley eventually accepted the Gorgos cup, not the Phintias one. I have not taken account of this in the preceding lines on the artist's career because I find it difficult to combine a career as a brilliant cup painter of about 510–500 with what seems to be a consistent development as a pot painter in later decades, while the Gorgos cup shows a degree of subtlety in narrative (Memnon's trapped spear, Eos' torn dress) not characteristic of the Berlin Painter's scenes, and (as Robertson himself has pointed out) Gorgos writes differently (tailing his R's). The case remains open.

Other pot painters

Not all the red figure pot painters of the Pioneer years had been great artists. The NIKOXENOS PAINTER was an adequate black figure painter of the Leagros Group who misguidedly took to red figure, painting Type A amphorae (and one of Type B, the old shape revived now), some of Panathenaic shape, hydriai, and some craters. Of these the Panathenaic are interesting for their corruption of the usual scene with Athena, changing her pose and the order of the columns [162], or substituting a Hermes or priest. His satyr athletes on [163] might also be conceived in a mocking spirit (their trainer uses a large phallos in place of a cane) or refer to a satyr play (Aeschylus' Isthmiastae). He has a distinctive way of drawing chiton sleeves and sometimes fails to make his drapery lines end where they should. He went on painting black figure, including Panathenaics, while his pupil, the EUCHARIDES PAINTER, carried on several of his tricks of drawing in red figure, like the ears with big round lobes, in a better style which runs on to the 470's. He prefers the new popular shapes – [164–7] neck amphorae, stamnoi, and the revived column crater, but has more ambitious work on calyx craters where, like his master, he may put figures on the lower bowl [166] as well as on the straight sides. The style is still angular and abrupt but his attempts on the subjects of his betters are far more successful.

Column craters had not been much in favour in the last quarter of the sixth century, but from about 500 they increasingly serve as stouter and more serviceable mixing bowls than the other crater types. They are rather old-fashioned in appearance, with base rays, and the necks black, or with a row of thin black buds, or ivy, or rarely with a row of silhouette animals or figures. In common with the treatment of scenes on other shapes, such as pelikai, the decorative panel frames are gradually abandoned, and the figures set in free field or on a ground line. They do not generally attract the best work.

MYSON [168–72] was a column crater specialist. He may have started with cups before 500 – one names Leagros. His signature, as potter and painter, is on a small column crater dedicated on the Acropolis [168] and showing Athena on either side, probably a gift of the artist. Some set-piece myth scenes show some originality of theme and solid, competent figures reminiscent of Phintias. The notable scenes are of Croesus on his funeral pyre [171], which is a rare illustration of a recent historical figure already becoming myth; a touching study of bewildered old age in a rescue of Aithra [172]; satyrs breaking up a tomb [169]; Herakles breaking up Nereus' house. More characteristic, perhaps, are his many other Dionysiac, komast and athlete studies – smallish heads, rather tight-lipped, with slim sharp noses. He is not always sure about anatomy – notice Apollo's back and chest on [172], and in common with several other artists of his rank he over-emphasises the spine with a double line. We may suspect a conservative resistance to new styles of drawing and the new moods expressed by his betters, but his following will prove more interesting.

A number of other second-line painters succumb to the interest in column craters, but also decorate a fuller range of the shapes favoured by their seniors. The HARROW PAINTER [173–5] is more than ordinarily competent, fond of neck amphorae, borrowing from contemporary black figure the decoration for the neck of [173], which approximates to Panathenaic shape. He clearly admired and may have copied the Berlin Painter. He rarely ventures outside genre scenes into myth and the satyrs in Hephaistos' forge [174] may illustrate a satyr play. The FLYING ANGEL PAINTER has a more engaging range of scenes [176–8], especially of satyrs, including their family life and introducing child satyrs to Greek art (he is named from the group on [177]), and of satyrs or women engaged with phalloi or phallos birds [176]. He decorates several of the fairly rare Type C amphorae. His heads tend to carry pointed, drooping lower lips. The GERAS PAINTER [179–81], a poorer artist, specialises in pelikai, especially of the 'modern' variety with no frames to the pictures. He offers a considerable range of Herakles scenes, new and old, and some unusual domestic scenes with satyrs. His name vase shows Herakles cudgelling Old Age (Geras). A contemporary, the MATSCH PAINTER, shows a more interesting confrontation of the hero and demon [182]. The ARGOS PAINTER is like the Geras Painter. I pick out one of the oddities of Greek vase painting from his hand, a rare study of a camel [183]. And the SIREN PAINTER offers careful but dull figure work including his rather hackneyed name vase [184] on the back of which are three oddly featured Erotes (the leader is called Himeros).

The TYSZKIEWICZ PAINTER is more pretentious [185–7], with stiff but well-composed scenes of myth, often on large vases, which bid for the narrative effect of, say, the Kleophrades Painter, but totally lack his subtlety. The florals of his name vase [186] recall the later Berlin Painter (but notice how centre leaves overlap tendrils) and some of his work is Early Classical. His heads tend to big, block-like noses with deep-set eyes, and he experiments with frontal and three-quarter views of faces. The TROILOS PAINTER is rather similar [188–90], also fond of elaborate dress borders and patterns, more lively, less precise. The half-open mouths of many of his figures look rather silly and one is more concerned for Triptolemos' balance on [189] than impressed by his divinity.

A series of vases, including both the finer craters, and the common pelikai and stamnoi, has been called by Beazley the SYLEUS SEQUENCE and presents problems of identity with four stylistic nuclei which might indicate different artists or different stages in the career of one or two artists. The names are the Painter of the Munich Amphora [191], the Gallatin Painter [192], the Diogenes Painter [193, 194], the Syleus Painter [195–8]. Shared stylistic features are double lines on the breast bone, parallel and then divergent, and the inverted arc which runs across and under the cross strokes of the chest for males. The first named is close to the Pioneers still in manner but not quality. The Diogenes Painter is the best of the series, still sharply Archaic in definition of anatomy and dress. The Syleus Painter does seem to present a new personality, with a greater interest in a good range of floral patterns, capable even of recalling the Berlin Painter's later work in single figures, but with some narrative power too: an artist whose imagination outpaced his skill. But the battles on the fat pointed amphora in Brussels [196] have some force and show good understanding of new poses. He sometimes uses thinned paint as eyeshadow for men [198].

The SYRISKOS GROUP, mainly of the 470's and little earlier, presents a similar problem. Beazley took the Copenhagen Painter [199–201] and the Syriskos Painter [202–4] as brothers – 'hard to tell apart', and faced by two fine skyphoi in a private collection preferred to invent a third, 'P. S. Painter' [205, 206]. Probably all go together, the Copenhagen Painter representing more academic work, mainly on stamnoi of distinctive and unpleasant profile (broad-mouthed, hunch-shouldered: [199]), the other vases, of mixed merit (including very good) offering a wider range. The name Syriskos comes from a potter who made a knucklebone vase (astragalos) for the painter [204]. But the potter Pistoxenos, who seems to have specialised in skyphoi of various types (including one for Epiktetos which places his early career), made the two skyphoi for our artist ('P. S. Painter'), and on each we read 'Pistoxenos Syriskos epoiesen' [205, 206]. This is a puzzle. That they are skyphoi is enough to indicate that it is *the* Pistoxenos at work. Was Syriskos a nickname, an alias – 'little Syrian': 'trusty stranger'? The skyphoi are finely painted, already Early Classical, but the drawing betrays several features linking them with other vases of the group – the florals (palmettes with pointed centre leaves and the lotuses), the blobby treatment of hair. A notable scene on a stamnos is of a recent historical event [199] – the murder of the tyrant Hipparchos (514 B C) – not myth but an act for which the slayers had acquired heroic status.

A feature of the group is some odd shapes – the knucklebone, the rare squat lekythoi, head vases, a round aryballos, and the use (as on some of these) of white ground for outline figure work. This appears on alabastra of the group too, and related is the plentiful (some forty known) GROUP OF THE NEGRO ALABASTRA (of the 480's) with negro figures [208], which though simple, are by no means repetitive. It is a negro, white ground, that the Syriskos Painter puts on a head vase. There are other, finer alabastra with Amazons [209].

The alabastra lead us to consideration of other small vases, especially lekythoi. The shape was extremely popular in black figure and there was an enormous output in the old technique through the first quarter of the fifth century, and later (*ABFH* pp. 146ff.). White ground was used on many of the vases and, especially in the workshop of the Sappho and Diosphos Painters, we find figures on the white ground rendered in a mixture of black figure and outline technique. Apart from this semi-outline work there is some in pure outline, flanked by palmettes. These Side-Palmette lekythoi ([210] Diosphos Work-shop) present a technique which can be immediately related to the outline drawing on white ground practised by artists otherwise committed to red figure, of which we shall see more on cups. The associations of the shape with black figure retarded use of the new technique upon it. One Pioneer, the GALES PAINTER [211], has left us two, but of the painters mentioned in this chapter only the Berlin Painter favoured the shape. The artists to be named now are influenced by him. A popular subject was Nike, whom we see also on lekythoi and other small vases by the DUTUIT PAINTER [207, 212], a minor artist otherwise more closely related to the lekythos painters, who at his best has some precise charm, and a distinctly summary way with dress on his lesser work; and by the TITHONOS PAINTER who had an eye for dress and hem patterns, and whose Oxford lekythos with another Nike is a fitting end piece for this section [213].

162 *Panathenaic amphora by the Nikoxenos Painter. Athena. H. 43·5*

163 *Volute crater (neck) by the Nikoxenos Painter. Satyr athletes*

164 Neck amphora by the
Eucharides Painter. H. 32

165 Belly amphora (Type A) by the Eucharides Painter.
Hermes and Argos

166 Calyx crater by the Eucharides
Painter. Mission to Achilles

167 Cup by the Eucharides Painter

168 *Column crater signed by Myson.
Athena and votary*

169 *Column crater by Myson. Satyrs
destroy a tomb. H. 44*

170 *Column crater by Myson. H. 51*

171 Belly amphora (Type A) by Myson.
Croesus on the pyre. H. 58·5

172.1, 2 Calyx crater by Myson. Apollo;
Rescue of Aithra. H. 40·5

173 Panathenaic amphora by the
Harrow Painter. Eros. H. 30

174 Column crater by the Harrow Painter. Satyrs in
Hephaistos' forge

175 Hydria by the Harrow Painter

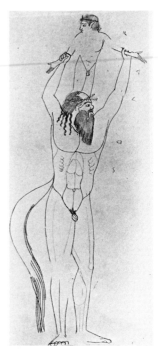

176 Belly amphora (Type C) by the Flying-Angel Painter.
Girl with phalloi and phallos-bird

177 Belly amphora (Type C) by the
Flying-Angel Painter (name vase)

178 Belly amphora (Type C) by the Flying-Angel
Painter

179 Pelike by the Geras Painter

180 Pelike by the
Geras Painter. H. 20

181 Volute crater by the Geras Painter.
Herakles and the Kerkopes

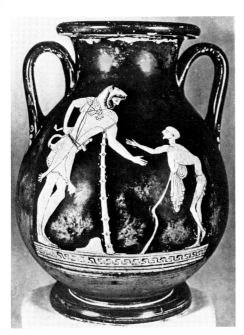

182 Pelike by the Matsch Painter.
Herakles and Geras

183 Pelike by the Argos Painter.
Negro and camel. H. 36

184.1 Stamnos by the Siren Painter (name vase). Odysseus and the
Sirens. H. 35.3

184.2 Reverse of 184.1. Erotes

185 Belly amphora by the Tyszkiewicz Painter.
Odysseus, Athena, Diomedes. H. 43·8

186 Calyx crater by the Tyszkiewicz Painter. Diomedes and Aeneas

187 Kalpis by the Tyszkiewicz Painter. Athena and Zeus fight giants

188 Calyx crater by the Troilos Painter. Athena's chariot with Herakles

189 Kalpis by the Troilos Painter. Triptolemos

190 Kalpis by the Troilos Painter (name vase).
Troilos and Polyxena

191 Belly amphora (Type A) by the Painter of the Munich Amphora (name vase)

192 Hydria by the Gallatin Painter. Danae

194 *Belly amphora by*
the Diogenes Painter

193 *Column crater by*
the Diogenes Painter. Zeus

195 *Stamnos by the Syleus Painter (name vase). Herakles and Syleus*

196 Pointed amphora by the Syleus Painter. Athena and Poseidon fight giants; centauromachy. H. 52

197 Pelike by the Syleus Painter. Apollo

198.1, 2 Stamnos by the Syleus Painter. Herakles and the Hydra. H. 65·3

199 Stamnos by the Copenhagen Painter. Death of Hipparchos

200 Hydria by the Copenhagen Painter. Medea rejuvenates 'Jason'

201 Stamnos by the Copenhagen Painter. Theseus and the Bull

*202 Column crater by the
Syriskos Painter. Hermes,
Zeus, Iris, Hera*

*203 Volute crater by the
Syriskos Painter. Eos and
Kephalos*

*204 Astragal vase by the
Syriskos Painter. Lion; Eros.
W. 17·5*

205 Skyphos by the P.S. Painter

206 Cup-skyphos by the P.S.
Painter. Theseus and Sinis

207 Oinochoe by the Dutuit
Painter

208 Alabastron of the Group of the Negro Alabastra. White ground. H. 16·2

209 Alabastron by the Painter of New York 21.131 (name vase). Amazon

210 Side-Palmette lekythos. Diosphos Workshop. White ground. H. 20·4

211 Lekythos by the Gales Painter. Procession to sacrifice. H. 31

212 Oinochoe by the Dutuit Painter. Artemis. H. 30

213 Lekythos by the Tithonos Painter. Nike. H. 35·1

Cup painters

Through the Late Archaic period, and especially in the first decade of the fifth century, at least half the production of red figure vases in Athens was accounted for by cups. This is a smaller proportion than the production of the later sixth century, when black figure artists still supplied most of the larger vases, but still considerably greater than in later years, when red figure artists answered all needs, although there was a growing production of plain black vases, and especially of black cups.

The old eye cup shape, Type A, is virtually dead. The elegant Type B and the heavier Type C with a concave rim are the popular forms, and a minor variety, the Acrocup [275] with a straight rim and either a shallow or a rounded bowl on a splaying foot with a moulding at its top, recalling features of the black figure Droop cup (*ABFH* pp. 61f.) whose long career was not yet over. The old scheme of decoration with eyes is quite gone except for very few examples by the Colmar and Antiphon Painters early in the century [242]. Even the palmette scrolls, with or without lotus terminals, become less common. But the tondos are regularly edged with a maeander pattern now, sometimes distinctively designed by different painters, and the same pattern quite often appears below the figure friezes.

The adoption of these pattern borders is a convenient signal for the advent of what we choose to call Late Archaic, but there is, of course, no sudden break, and just as we have had to trace in the last chapter the work of some painters well into the fifth century (as Epiktetos), so here several will praise Leagros and declare the start of their careers before the turn of the century. Indeed, before we turn to the more prolific great names, an isolated master-piece of little before 500 can provide a link. It is a superb cup in Berlin [214], signed by PEITHINOS (we have a scrap of another, earlier cup signed by him) and praising Athenodotos, whom we shall meet again. We have the new patterns in and out, a maeander echoed by the pattern of Peleus' locked hands as he grasps Thetis, unperturbed by her snakes and lion which attack him. Outside are lovers, more forward where their own sex is concerned, limbs showing clear through dress, with a display of spreading folds and zigzag hems recalling Phintias or the Sosias Painter.

There are one or two points of technique to be mentioned before we turn to the major cup painters. Coral-red for decoration of bands in or outside cups is still used, sparingly. There are, however, from about 510 on, a number of cups which employ white ground for the interior, occasionally for the exterior too. On these the decoration is in outline, using the same thick and thin painted lines with increasing use of added washes or red as time passes. We have noticed the technique on lekythoi (but no earlier), where outline and black figure can be mixed and it had become commonly used as a background for black figure on lekythoi and other shapes. Pamphaios made a cup with a black figure rider on the white ground tondo. Of the same date is a cup interior with an outline Dionysos facing a black figure satyr [215]. The cup is as early as any lekythos with comparable decoration, the style still Pioneer, and the attribution to Euphronios could be correct, but is not sure. The Gotha cup had white ground outside only [51]. The main series begins with cups of early Onesimos (Proto-Panaitian and the related Eleusis Painter [217] who still praises Leagros) and his kin [216], and continues in our period with examples by the Brygos Painter [218] and Douris among others [273]. The commonest scheme is to have a black border to the tondo, sometimes with a line farther in to frame the figure or figures. It becomes commoner to fill the interior with white, and the inner line border is then normal. If a ground line is needed it is usually an ovolo. A very few keep the red figure tondo but fill the zone round it with white to the lip. Exteriors are usually red figure, sometimes all black, occasionally white ground.

These are exquisite cups, usually avoiding the trivial in their subject-matter and often intended for dedication, showing deities or myth scenes. There is a distinguished succession in the Early Classical. Another dedicatory masterpiece is represented by a cup fragment from the Acropolis (no. 247) where the lines and figures are in flat, low relief, all gilt except for flesh and added white.

ONESIMOS [222–35] signs one cup [228] made for him by Euphronios, whose own painting career was by then over. Some ten other cups made by Euphronios are painted by Onesimos or artists of his studio, so we can regard this as a single workshop – or bench within a workshop. While Onesimos' style is readily definable from his signed vase the earlier stages of his career remain problematic, since his style develops from a fine late sixth-century group of cups related to Pioneer work (recall Euphronios the painter's cups). Beazley came to agree with earlier scholars that works assembled for a Panaitios Painter were by Onesimos, and that he emerges from a late sixth-century Proto-Panaitian Group. The associations are still open to discussion.

Most of the Proto-Panaitian cups [220, 221] carry the new maeander borders, in and out. They are free with kalos names (another Pioneer trait) naming Leagros, Athenodotos (as does Peithinos), Epidromos and Panaitios among others. The style is 'reduced' Pioneer with some elaboration of features and anatomy on larger figures, some drooping mouth corners, dress and limb arrangements (notice the odd frontal toes for a reclining figure [220]) of their day. Subjects are almost exclusively komos and athletics.

The Panaitian vases, mainly of 505–485, reduce the use of maeander outside – which is a general tendency in this period, away from the Archaic florals and borders on cups – and they confess devotions similar to those of their fore-runners – to Leagros and Athenodotos. There is a robust narrative style here, with lithe darting figures, skilfully composed and balanced on the broad arc of the cup. [223] is the best example with pairs of Theseus encounters outside, and a tondo inside with young Theseus, supported by a merman (Triton), receiving the crown from Amphitrite, with Athena beyond. The goddess' swaying figure and the fish give a vivid impression of an underwater setting despite the conventions of red figure which rather act against any such atmosphere. Our artist is particularly good at facial characterisations of balding komasts or satyrs. Even his figures in repose are instinct to their fingertips with immanent life. Anatomically he moves away from Pioneer pattern to clear linear statements of most varied poses: a favourite is the twisting back view, with distinctive broken V shoulder blades and sometimes the double spine. He is bolder with frontal faces [227] than his contemporaries and on profiles usually has a sulky drooping line at mouth corners. He observes life,

and at last a girl's breasts are shown properly: the outline running into the armpit is an observed feature [224, 225] while before the profile 'breast symbols' were imposed on the body unrealistically. The Doris (=Douris) on the girl's cup on [225] names her more probably than the vase painter. There is other realistic observation of detail – notably in body hair and genitals. The vases which are assembled around Onesimos' signed cup [224, 228–32] differ from the foregoing slightly in style, subject and date. Panaitios is still kalos, but now also Lykos and Erothemis. Maeander borders are sometimes dropped, and some round tondos are interrupted by 'teeth' (compare [243]: making a reserved battlement pattern), crosses or chequer squares. Running varieties of maeander are preferred now to the stopt (cross lines running to the border). The interest in myth and even satyr subjects has waned, and they are replaced by horsemen and athletes (several wearing exercise caps [227]). The figures themselves, even the girls, look more boyish, with slim figures, small features beneath bushy fringed hair. There is a lightness to the scenes which never becomes merely trivial, but whether this can represent the late maturity of the Proto-Panaitian artist remains difficult to affirm.

There are some lesser artists to be mentioned before our next master. The BONN and COLMAR PAINTERS are early, working from before 500 to the 480's, the former specialising in centaurs and fights, the latter in athletes and symposia, generally avoiding much myth. The Bonn Painter [237] still incises some hair outlines and has some Oltan profiles and florals. The Colmar Painter [236, 238] shares Onesimos' affection for Leagros and Panaitios and some of his later cups may have been decorated for the potter Euphronios. Both painters (and Beazley was not sure about separating them) achieve a certain prettiness: notice the patterning, florals and circumstantial detail of the deer hunt on [237], and lifelike expression if dull dress on [238].

The ANTIPHON PAINTER [239–43] is a more substantial figure, named for the kalos on an unusual slender stand [239]. His work resembles the Panaitian but is heavier, duller, sometimes simply cruder and permits us to appreciate Onesimos' delicacy the better. Komasts, athletes and warriors are his subjects, rarely myth, and he shares with Onesimos admiration for Lykos and Aristarchos. This, and his use of 'teeth' to interrupt tondo maeanders [243], place his *floruit* with mature Onesimos in the 480's. His figures have big heads, the anatomy dull but plausible with torsos split lengthwise by a black (broken) line rather than divided at chest level. Old-fashioned are his occasional use of incision to outline hair, which otherwise often looks curly with a heavily scalloped edge (an effect enhanced by a border of not-quite-relief blobs of paint), and some eye cup schemes with small under-handle palmettes [242]. He was a prolific artist and there are many unassigned cups in his manner or related to his work. The CAGE PAINTER can be named beside him [244].

Brygos' signature as potter appears on over a dozen cups, on the edge of the base or on the plain under-handle. Almost all were decorated by the BRYGOS PAINTER [218, 245–61] or artists of his circle, the master being the most prolific with well over two hundred vases now attributed to him. He decorates few other shapes, including skyphoi [248, 259], head kantharoi and rhyta [257, 258], a big kalathoid jar with a spout [261] and several lekythoi [249]. His cups are Types B's and Type C's, the former including some with a distinctive cone foot, the latter usually omitting the maeander base line. Around the tondos the maeander is usually stopt, often interrupted by cross in square or knobbed X's. He paints a few white ground cup interiors ([218]: exterior [256]), and a white ground lekythos.

His style derives from that of the early Onesimos, and his main period of work lies in the 480's and 470's, the later vases being mainly small cups with pictures inside only and the lekythoi. There is weakness in his later work, but in his prime his vigour and invention are unparalleled. What is sometimes missed in subtlety of line is more than made up for in expressiveness of features and in pose. Of all Archaic artists he demonstrates best the new command of pose based on observation and quite independent of the stock repertory of figures in action or quiet. His is 'one of the first, one of the only, real children in vase painting' (Beazley) [259] and in many of his scenes, genre and myth, we catch this sure delineation of the varying ages of men and women – for example all the figures on the Priam skyphos [248]. For the

135

Sappho on the big spouted jar (a very late work, if his at all) he experiments with a three-quarter face [261]. What greater painters like the Kleophrades Painter achieved they executed in a more conventional idiom. This is why the Brygos Painter is at his most characteristic in his favourite symposion or athlete scenes where he could exercise his command at portrayal of the everyday gesture or situation. It is arguable that Greek art never quite recaptured this freshness. His heads are not easily forgotten – the flat tops, high brows over narrow eyes, long nose line. The mouths are always expressive, bellowing song, puffed at the pipes, or tight-lipped. His men are often balding, often hairy, and typically Brygan are the stubble head and beard of the senile. His use of thinned paint approaches real painting, and goes beyond varied linear effects. On his vases and those of his companions there are several examples of shading suggesting the roundness of shields: [248] cf. [268]. A feature of some tondos is the splaying composition of two-figure groups: [245] cf. [255].

His myth scenes are equally original – the unique dead Ajax covered by Tekmessa [246] and a variety of other scenes especially involving Achilles (Briseis, and the quarrel over his armour [247]), as well as the famous Ransom of Hector on the Vienna skyphos [248]. In the Dionysiac scenes the god himself enters more into the spirit of his troupe than usual [255]. On [252] he appears warily on the scene of his satyrs' attempted rape of Iris and Hera. Iris relies on her wings for escape: Hera on the diplomacy of Hermes backed by Herakles' bow. The satyrs are brilliant studies of lust, overt and stealthy, of surprise, of expected satisfaction. The inscriptions, so far as they are intelligible, both label and comment, and on other cups our painter's figures are seen to sing or cry out with real legends. Surprisingly, kalos inscriptions are extremely rare, but the painter was not single-minded in his choice of love themes.

A number of other cup painters are of the Brygos Painter's Circle, some no lesser artists than the master but less prolific, less influential, and there can be little doubt to whom is owed the common stock of figures, poses and subjects, even much of the details of anatomy and dress. The FOUNDRY PAINTER [262–8] – 'an excellent artist: with his forcible, sometimes even brutal, style he often equals the Brygos Painter' (Beazley) – has a distinctive personality.

His figures, though Brygan, are heavier set, the features often more lightly sketched (straight, not arched brows), but carefully observed and we have good studies of oafish lovers, dismayed roués, buxom wenches [265]. He details muscle and body hair, and on [266] and [268] we have rare examples in this period of shading. His symposia have the spirit of the Brygos Painter, but detail and pose are often original. He takes an original view of myth too, but is perhaps remembered best for his depiction of craftsmen – the bronze sculptors' workshop from which he takes his name [262], with the furnace being stoked and blown (the boy behind with bellows), the statue assembled, and on the other side another being scraped down and finished. Another vase shows a marble sculptor, watched over by Athena [264].

Two other followers of Brygos are excellent artists but lack the master's vigour – 'mild Brygan' Beazley called them. The heads of their figures are far wider-eyed, blander, their action figures seem rehearsed rather than spontaneous in their movements, and the second of them in particular is nervous in his use of broken lines in dress, sometimes discordantly angular (especially on larger figures), sometimes affectedly billowing. The first is the BRISEIS PAINTER [270–3] who likes the wing sleeves for his dancing maenads [271] and is generally fond of scenes with women at various domestic occasions. His name vase offers another of the novel views of the Iliad, so popular in these years, with Briseis led away from a sulking Achilles [270]. The DOKIMASIA PAINTER [274–7] is generally quieter still, preferring a stock range of komos scenes and studies of young men with horses – his name derives from the annual inspection of cavaliers and their mounts conducted by the Athenian Council and apparently shown on his name vase, where a scribe is present. Both painters decorate larger vases too. The Dokimasia Painter is the more interesting with two stamnoi showing a spirited slaughter of Orpheus by the Thracian women [277], and a fine calyx crater in Boston with the deaths of Agamemnon and Aigisthos on either side [274]. The Agamemnon, with the king enveloped in a cloth, recalls Aeschylus' treatment of the story, but on conventional dating the vase is earlier than the production of the *Agamemnon* (458 B C) and we should therefore suppose this version of the story to be the invention of an earlier poet. The Dokimasia Painter, at least, is working still in the 460's.

The PAINTER OF LOUVRE G 265 is another mild (and late) Brygan, but slipshod [278], and the PAINTER OF THE PARIS GIGANTOMACHY more vigorous and prolific [279, 280].

The painter DOURIS [281–300] appears to have been at least as productive as the Brygos Painter, with some three hundred vases attributed to him. He signs thirty-nine vases as painter, one of them also as potter, and another as potter alone. In early days he worked for Kleophrades and, it seems, Euphronios, but throughout his career he was working for the potter Python, whose name appears alone on the plain side of three cup feet. Douris' name was often taken in vain, or very popular. We saw it written on the cup carried by a girl on a cup by Onesimos [225], and the Cartellino Painter writes it on a ticket on one vase and on the dress of figures on others; then there is the 'forgery' on the Triptolemos Painter's cup, yet to be noticed.

Douris was a painter of considerable efficiency, charm and dullness. Sometimes his slim, distinctively round-headed figures carry an aura of Archaic innocence and one cannot but admire the energy and the impartiality with which he visits but rarely enhances every genre subject known to the Late Archaic artist. In his later work his prettiness becomes merely slick and there seemed no reason why he should ever stop turning out his rather mechanical and shallow paintings. His long career runs from about 500 to near 460 and his mood must have chimed well with the new Early Classical.

Beazley distinguished four main periods in his work by criteria which I summarise below, adding observations on changes in style and subject interest:

(I)   [281–4] This sees Douris at his best with no less promise than Onesimos beside whom he may have sat. There is a tendency to the ornate in the varieties of border pattern, including the palmette friezes which appeared on some of the great late sixth-century cups, and twice he adds a figure frieze round a tondo. Some tondo compositions and myth scenes have a quality of monumentality which would not have disgraced the finer pot painters of the day. His mouths are particularly expressive, often with sharply downturned lower lips (note the contrast on [283]). In this, and the next period, Chairestratos is the favoured kalos name.

(II) [285–7, 299] The decorative strain thins and most tondos have no borders now, but for rare experiment with varieties of single maeander elements alternating with squares. An odd feature is the way he now begins to give a bold hook to the inner end of collar bones. Generally this is an early feature but Douris emphasises it later in his career (the Brygos Painter and his Circle, and Makron ignored it). Scenes with youths and athletes seem now preferred to the earlier drinking parties.

138

(III) [288–94] Tondo borders now carry the distinctive Dourian single maeander and square patterns. There is commonly a palmette complex at each cup handle, and where the tondo has a ground line the area below is left plain. Hippodamas is the favourite kalos name. This is Douris at his most characteristic and recognisable, though not at his best. He loves full curves of transparent drapery. Thick black hemlines are preferred and we begin to see the late patterning of grouped lines on dress. He has been thought responsible for an interest in back views of symposiasts [290] but he is not otherwise particularly inventive in posture. The symposion regains its place as a prime subject, together with studies of warriors and of youths at school [289] (including mythical later, with Herakles attacking his tutor Linos [296]: notice that the hero, though young, is already fierce-eyed).

(IV) [295–7] The late vases signal a return to the ornate. The tondo borders by now have two maeander elements between the squares, not one, and as well as the handle palmette we see now more lotuses, usually with separated leaves which seem especially Dourian, and even floating blossoms in the field. Most of his studies of women seem late. Dress has the grouped lines more often, with simpler hems, and on males the hooked collar bones are seen more rarely.

His myth scenes appear throughout his career, with no perceptible pattern. There are some oddities, like the dragon regurgitating Jason [288] with the golden fleece hanging beyond and Athena watching with her owl. This is a unique variant on the Argonaut story. He decorates a few other shapes. His earliest signed work, probably before 500, is a round aryballos [282]. Of his lekythoi, one white ground example recently recovered carried an exceptionally, excessively ornate Atalanta [294], still running though in her Sunday best. The London psykter [299] is deservedly famous for its versatile satyrs at a party or from a satyr play (one dressed as Hermes). His literacy is many sided: from the epic verse on the scroll in the school scene [289] to the lover's whisper to his lass in a tense situation – 'keep still' [297]. Douris was influential in the Early Classical period. Very close to him in his latest work is the OIDIPUS PAINTER, whose name vase I show [301]: hero and sphinx within, a satyr family on the outside, with a child perhaps being chastened for the empty wine jar being tested on the left.

The TRIPTOLEMOS PAINTER [302–7] is an accomplished and versatile artist who started as a cup painter but soon turned to decorate the full range of larger vessels, especially pelikai, stamnoi and column craters, favoured by major painters of the day. It is for the larger vases that he reserves his studies of myth and Beazley admired his 'accomplished, strong, pure', expression of Late Archaic art. His cups, including some with robust erotic subjects [302], have more of Douris than the Brygos Painter in them. His early work need hardly date earlier than the 480's, and the Edinburgh cup with Greeks fighting Persians on foot and horseback (the Easterners shooting from their mounts, even to the rear) must illustrate recent Athenian successes [*303*]. His later work, including most of his larger vases, is already Early Classical, of about 470. On an amphora of Panathenaic shape Athena is acting as scorer in the games, with stylus and writing tablet open [*307*]. Other myth scenes and figures may be as late but remain soberly Archaic in mood and execution; mysterious too, like the ram labelled 'Pat[roklos]' fought over by Ajax and Hector [*304*]. Both painting and potting link his work with Douris and a cup that he paints is signed as though painted by Douris. This is not a case of identity of artists, nor is it very likely that they had the same name. It might be an ancient forgery within the workshop, or a compliment paid by the senior painter.

MAKRON [*308–18*] claims some three hundred and fifty attributed vases, the most prolific or well preserved of all early red figure artists. He signs only one, possibly two, vases as painter, and seems to have worked exclusively for the potter Hieron whose signature appears on over thirty of his vases, usually incised or painted on the handles. His is a far rougher hand than Douris', his figures heavier, but on some of his best works – especially skyphoi [*308, 309*] – where he is careful too, the effect can be impressive and calm. His heads tend to a low brow and flat skull, and he is fond of hair in separate locks, suggesting brunette or blonde, for both men and women. On the best vases he loves detailing decoration, often figured, on furniture, dresses and skins [*309, 311*]. He is best at women's dress, expressing the billowing folds on dancing figures and rendering even the serpentine hems of close hanging folds with care and variety. Compare the maenads' dress on his Berlin cup [*311*] with the dull precision of these details on much contemporary work. For cup tondos he admitted only the regular maeander as border. Some cup handles get a framework of reserved-heart palmettes, some plus spiky leaved lotuses, or an occasional ivy branch beneath them. His early work is less fully decorated.

Myth claims few of his vases, and on these the Trojan cycle outnumbers all others, but there are no markedly original compositions, except for individual figures which have a certain casual ease. Most of his other vases carry groups of men, women and youths, dancing or passing the time of day together with a number of the usual Dionysiac, symposion and athlete subjects. Among others he names Hippodamas and Hiketes as kalos, names familiar from Douris' later career. Makron was a younger man, probably working – and working hard! – mainly in the 480's and a little later.

214.1 Cup signed by Peithinos. Peleus and Thetis

214.2, 3 outside of 214.1

215 Cup. White ground. Dionysos and satyr

216 Cup in the manner of
Onesimos. White ground.
Herakles

217 Cup by the Eleusis
Painter. White ground.
Triton

218 Cup by the Brygos
Painter. White ground. See
256 for outside

219 *Cup near the Eleusis Painter*

220 *Cup, Proto-Panaitian*

221 *Cup, Proto-Panaitian*

222 *Cup by Onesimos*

223.1 *Cup by Onesimos. Theseus visits Amphitrite*

223.2 *Outside of 223.1. Theseus with Skiron and Procrustes*

224 Cup by Onesimos

225 Cup by Onesimos

226 Cup by Onesimos

227.1, 2 Cup by Onesimos

228 Cup signed by Onesimos

229 Cup by Onesimos. Negro groom

230 Cup by Onesimos

231 Cup by Onesimos. Herakles and the sons of Eurytos

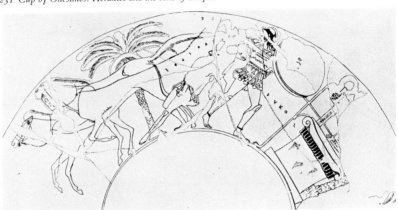

232 Cup by Onesimos. Achilles kills Troilos

233 Cup by Onesimos

234 Kyathos by Onesimos. Reading. H. 10·5

235 Cup by Onesimos. Trainer
with pen and tablet

236 Cup by the Colmar Painter

237 Cup by the Bonn Painter. Deerhunt

238 Cup by the Colmar Painter

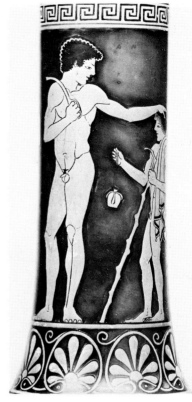

239 Stand by the Antiphon
Painter (name vase)

240 Cup by the Antiphon
Painter. Boar hunt

241 Cup by the Antiphon Painter

242 Cup by the Antiphon Painter. W. 31

243 Cup by the Antiphon Painter

244 Cup by the Cage Painter (name vase)

245.1 *Cup by the Brygos Painter. Phoinix and Briseis*

245.2 *Outside of 245.1. Death of Priam*

246 Cup by the Brygos Painter. Ajax dead

247 Cup by the Brygos Painter. Quarrel over the armour of Achilles

248 Skyphos by the Brygos
Painter. Ransom of Hector

249 Lekythos by the Brygos Painter.
Athena with aphlaston. H. 34

250 Cup by the Brygos Painter. Klytaimnestra

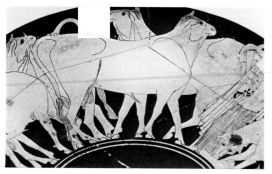

251 Cup by the Brygos Painter. Hermes with the cattle of Apollo

252.1 Cup by the Brygos Painter. Satyrs attack Hera. W. 27.5

252.2 Reverse of 252.1. Satyrs attack Iris

253.1–3 Cup by the Brygos Painter. W. 32

254. Cup by the Brygos Painter

255 Cup by the Brygos
Painter. Dionysos

256 Cup by the Brygos Painter. Dionysos. See 218 for inside

257 *Rhyton (neck) by the Brygos Painter*

258 *Rhyton (neck) by the Brygos Painter. Pygmies and cranes*

259 *Skyphos by the Brygos Painter*

260 *Cup by the Brygos Painter*

261 *Kalathoid vase by the Brygos Painter. Alcaeus and Sappho. H. 25·3*

262.1 *Cup by the Foundry Painter (name vase).*
Hephaistos and Thetis

262.2, 3 *Outside of 262.1.*
Sculptors' workshop. W. 30·5

263 Cup by the Foundry
Painter. Pankration

264 Cup by the Foundry
Painter. Sculptor

265 Cup by the Foundry
Painter

266 Cup by the Foundry Painter

267 Oinochoe by the Foundry Painter. White ground. Woman spinning. H. 22·2

268 Cup by the Foundry Painter

269 Cup by the Foundry Painter (?). Theseus deserts Ariadne

270 *Cup by the Briseis Painter (name vase). Briseis led from Achilles*

271.1, 2 *Cup by the Briseis Painter*

272 *Cup by the Briseis Painter*

273 *Cup by the Briseis Painter. White ground*

274.1, 2 Calyx crater by the Dokimasia Painter. Death of Agamemnon; Death of Aigisthos. H. 51

275.1, 2 Cup (Acrocup) by the
Dokimasia Painter. H. 14·5

276 Cup by the Dokimasia
Painter. Dolon

277 Stamnos by the Dokimasia
Painter. Death of Orpheus

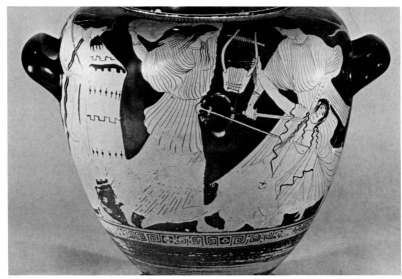

278 *Cup by the Painter of Louvre G 265*

279 *Cup by the Painter of the Paris Gigantomachy. Greek and Persians*

280.1 *Cup by the Painter of the Paris Gigantomachy (name vase). Poseidon and giant*

280.2 *Outside of 280.1. Gods (Dionysos) and giants*

285.1 *Cup signed by Douris. Voting for the armour of Achilles. W. 33·8*

285.2 *Interior of 285.1. Odysseus receives armour of Achilles*

286 *Cup signed by Douris*

287 *Cup signed by Douris. Theseus and the Krommyonian sow and Sinis*

288 Cup by Douris. Jason disgorged by the dragon; Athena. W. 30

289 Cup signed by Douris. School

291 Cup by Douris

290 Cup signed
by Douris

292 Cup signed by Douris. Eos and Memnon

293 Cup by Douris

294 Lekythos by Douris. Atalanta. H. 31·8

295.1 Cup by Douris.
Prometheus and Hera

295.2 Outside of 295.1.
Return of Hephaistos

296 Cup by Douris. Herakles and Linos

297 Cup by Douris

298 Kantharos (Type C) signed by Douris. Herakles and Amazons. H. 18·2

299.1, 2 Psykter signed by Douris

300 Cup in the manner of Douris. Herakles in the bowl of the Sun

301.1 Cup by the Oidipus Painter

301.2 Interior of 301.1.
Oidipus and the Sphinx

302 Cup by the Triptolemos Painter

303.1 Cup by the Triptolemos Painter

303.2 Outside of 303.1. Greeks and Persians

304.1 Stamnos by the Triptolemos Painter. Mission to Achilles

304.2 Reverse of 304.1. Ajax and Hector

305 Cup by the Triptolemos Painter

306 Calyx crater by the
Triptolemos Painter. Danae and the
rain of Zeus. H. 41

307.1 Panathenaic amphora by the
Triptolemos Painter. Athena and tablet.
H. 43·5

307.2 Reverse of 307.1. Athlete,
infibulated

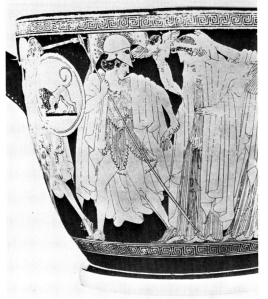

308.1 *Skyphos signed by Makron. Paris leads Helen.*
H. 21·5

308.2 *Reverse of 308.1. Menelaos recovers Helen*

309 *Skyphos by Makron.*
Demeter and
Triptolemos. H. 21

310 Cup by Makron. Judgement of Paris. W. 37

311 Cup by Makron. Worship of Dionysos

312 Cup by Makron. W. 32·5

313 Cup by Makron

314 Cup by Makron. Satyr player

315 Cup by Makron

316 *Askos by Makron. Erotes. W. 10*

317 *Cup by Makron*

318.1, 2 *Aryballos by Makron. Boys with toy chariots. H. 6·1*

Chapter Four

MANNERISTS AND OTHERS

It is not possible to take the full measure of the Early Classical style in red figure in this book, but merely to introduce it and to study the last throes of Archaism before the mid fifth century. The period is one which sees a considerable increase in activity in the potters' quarter, with more numerous exports to North and South Italy (albeit fewer to Etruria after the defeat of the Etruscans at Cumae by the Greeks of Syracuse and Cumae in about 474 B C), and stylistically a growing dependence on the example of major painting in Greek sanctuaries and public buildings. We have entered the period when painters were for the first time famous artists in antiquity – but still not the vase painters. The new mood and themes of the Early Classical cannot be fully studied here nor the effects of major painting, but something of the new manners in drawing can. All the groups presented depend, in varying degrees, on the Archaic. The Mannerists indulge the patterns of Archaic, without its heart, with the exception of one master, the Pan Painter, and the pot and cup painters chosen are pupils, imitators or followers of the greater Late Archaic artists, not themselves masters, but bearing sufficient indication for us of the new styles better practised by others.

Mannerists

The Early Classical style expresses a new ethos to which Archaic delight in patterns of anatomy or dress contributes nothing, but which could build on Archaic experiment in subtlety of pose and composition to render mood or emotion. But the patterns of Archaism were not quickly abandoned and centuries later they could still inform a vigorous sculptural style. In the 470's the exhaustion of Archaism and the promise of new styles left artists with a choice between commitment to the new, or the continuation of the old, where, with the heart gone, only the trappings could still entertain. All the old artists were affected by the change and become 'sub-Archaic' in their later work, notably those who had best expressed the Late Archaic mood, even the Berlin Painter. Others, and their pupils, who remained committed to the old have been called 'Mannerists' because some of the qualities of their work are recalled by Mannerist movements in other periods of art. Physically this sub-

Archaic Mannerism may be rendered by slimmer figures, smaller heads, exaggeration of gesture, exploitation of pattern in dress for its own sake with little regard to the natural forms which had inspired the Archaic schemes; in mood it is rendered by triviality of subject, with a touch of the theatrical (in the modern sense) in the treatment of myth. There were traces of Mannerism in the work of some artists already before 480 and we can see which workshop bred its most devoted adherents. These we consider first. One major artist, the Pan Painter, made a virtue of Mannerism, and his work is in a totally different class, but it is a symptom of the same last flourish of what was probably the most fruitful and exciting period of red figure vase painting in Athens.

The Mannerists are painters mainly of column craters, pelikai and hydriai (kalpides). On these the scenes are generally framed with the old black ivy patterns, and with rows of black buds as borders, on crater necks, pelikai or between the hydria handles. Dionysiac or komos and symposion scenes account for most of their painting, with a few, generally old-fashioned, myths. The shapes, patterns and many scenes are those of Myson, and at his bench the early Mannerists learned their craft. The PIG PAINTER [319–21] is one of the first and Beazley found it not easy to say where he begins and Myson ends. For a demonstration of Mannerism look at the illogical wavy borders to the man's himation on [320] and the boy's proportions. Notice his special amphora shape [319]. The LENINGRAD PAINTER [322–6] can manage narrative better but the emaciation of the figures on [324] is rivalled only by that of the vase itself. His vase workshop, visited by Nikai (notice the swing of their dress) and Athena is an important scene, not least for the woman craftsman at the right [323]. 'Not an average day in the Mannerist workshop' remarked Beazley, apropos of the vase shapes, but details of shape and disposition of pattern suggest that this is a metal-vase studio, with chasing and gilding in progress. The satyr cabinet-makers on [325] probably illustrate Aeschylus' satyr play, the *Thalamopoioi*.

Other early Mannerists of yet slighter quality represented here are the AGRIGENTO PAINTER [327, 328], OINANTHE PAINTER [329] and PERSEUS PAINTER [330] with some pieces unattached [331–4]. Some of these works must be as late as the 450's and they have successors, to the end of the century, not considered here. It is interesting to notice that the vases found a stronger market in Italy (except Etruria) than most of their contemporaries.

Beside these the PAN PAINTER is a paragon [335–49]. Though with some preference for the Mannerist shapes he also decorates the fullest possible range of vases including many lekythoi (some white ground), cups, some amphorae and a series of cult loutrophoroi. His range of subjects is unrivalled – all types of genre, myth scenes and figures restated or invented. Among these we may pick out several of sacrifice [340] or with religious themes, but our artist is no puritan [346]. If Myson's followers have lent the term 'Mannerist' a pejorative meaning, then the Pan Painter deserves some other epithet and it is a pity that Beazley's 'sub-Archaic' has not won support. He was working already by about 480, his treatment of Archaic composition and pattern then perhaps rather precious, as on the Marpessa vase [338]. Later he clings to the subsidiary patterns and florals of Late Archaism, notably eclectic in border patterns and elaborated lotuses including the newly revived straight-sided variety, and he gives some palmette leaves spines. The ovolo too is by now a commoner border pattern. His best scenes have a unique theatricality in the best sense, being an improvement on life. You can almost hear the bustle and the chatter, while the degree of affectation in dress or gesture renders the scenes no less vivid. His drawing is distinctive. Proportions tend to the slim, but not excessively, and the Archaic patterns of dress are varied but seldom illogical with folds ending in arcs or wavy lines, not zigzags. His heads are small, round, with full chins, short noses, thick necks, beady eyes. He is careful with anatomy detail, often adding expressive extra lines and arcs on arms and necks. The hook of the collar bones is sometimes detached. Fissures in rocks are elegantly stylised [335, 344].

His name vase, a bell crater in Boston, must have been painted in the 460's, probably early [335]. It gives us Pan, inspired by a rustic idol to pursue a yokel: a new subject, a comparatively new god for Attic art. Observe the three heads – mortal booby, animal divinity, pop-eyed symbol of country matters. Notice how the artist uses his brush – the cap, goatskin cloak, Pan's beard, rocks. On the other side Artemis threatens with her bow as she sweeps past Aktaion, torn by his dogs, an arm flung up in agony. There has been nothing in the conventions of red figure to lead us to believe that such a mood or composition was possible or even admissible. But, for affectation notice the slimness of the goddess and the tiny dogs; contrast the stacked multiple zigzags of Artemis' himation, with the shaken-out folds of her skirt, with the interlocking hook folds on Aktaion's cloak, and then recall the swirling pattern of the boy's dress on the other side of the vase. This is pattern for pattern's sake, but diverse and subordinated to figure and theme. We have an earlier treatment of the Aktaion story by our artist [337.1], where he gives the hunter a deerskin body-stocking for his dogs to worry and tear.

The Athens pelike with Herakles fighting the servants of Busiris [336] may be a little earlier than the Pan vase, and is no less dramatic in mood. Novel

319 Neck amphora by the Pig Painter. Theseus and Procrustes. H. 34

320 Column crater by the Pig Painter

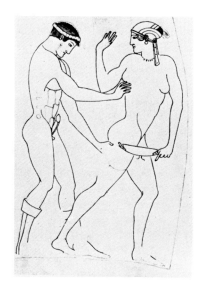

321 Column crater by the Pig Painter

322 Column crater by the Leningrad Painter

323 Kalpis by the Leningrad Painter. Vase workshop

325 Kalpis by the Leningrad Painter. Satyr players

324 Neck amphora by the Leningrad Painter.
Nike and lyreplayer. H. 50

326 Kalpis by the Leningrad Painter. Lapiths (Kaineus)
and centaurs

327 Kalpis by the Agrigento Painter.
Hermes, Argos and Io

328 Kalpis by the Agrigento Painter.
Music lesson

329 Kalpis by the Oinanthe Painter.
Birth of Erichthonios

330 *Pelike-by the Perseus Painter. Herm. H. 20*

331 *Kalpis, Mannerist. Seven against Thebes arming*

332 *Pelike, Mannerist. Achilles receives new armour*

333 *Column crater, Mannerist. Chorus for Dionysos. H. 40·5*

334 *Lekythos, Mannerist. H. 39·2*

335.1 Bell crater by the Pan Painter (name vase). Pan and boy. H. 37·1

335.2 Reverse of 335.1. Artemis and Aktaion

336 Pelike by the Pan Painter. Herakles and Busiris

337.1 Volute crater by the Pan Painter. Artemis and Aktaion

337.2 Reverse of 337.1. Dionysos and giant

338.1, 2 Psykter by the Pan Painter. Apollo fights Idas for Marpessa

340 Column crater by the Pan Painter.
Sacrifice at a herm

341 Oinochoe by the Pan Painter.
Boreas and Oreithyia

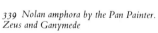

339 Nolan amphora by the Pan Painter.
Zeus and Ganymede

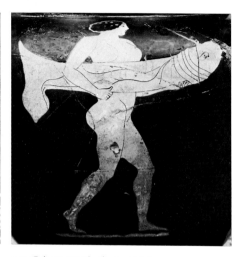

342 Column crater by the Pan Painter

343 Bell crater by the Pan Painter. Dionysos

344 Pelike by the Pan Painter

345 Nolan amphora by the Pan Painter. Nereid

346 *Dinos by the Pan Painter*

347 *Lekythos by the Pan Painter*

348 *Lekythos by the Pan Painter. Nike. H. 35*

349 *Pelike by the Pan Painter. Perseus with gorgoneion*

observation again – the bald, circumcised Africans, and indulgence in architectural pattern on the altar. Gestures are exaggerated no further than is required to demonstrate the barbarians' dismay. Comparable qualities are discernible in other action scenes where Archaic vigour is enhanced by this new, sophisticated flair with line and dress.

His latest work lacks bite (as [*341, 344, 346*]), the sharp relief line is less regularly used and there is a reversion to more formal Archaic pattern, but self-conscious now and more truly mannered. 'The painter begins as a mannerist, and ends as a mannerist. Between he is more' (Beazley). The Mannerists are an art-historical curiosity, but the Pan Painter delivered Archaic Greek art's last statement of pattern and action in an Athens where muralists, vase painters and, soon, sculptors were working towards the new Classical idealism. He could have no followers of quality in such a climate but it was fitting that the last great exponent of the Archaic was also one of its masters.

Pot painters

The stamnos had been an important shape in the first quarter of the century and it long remains so although major artists still prefer the larger craters and we do not know enough about the uses of the stamnos to be sure that it always served any radically different purpose from them. [*350*] is a fine Early Classical example by an artist who must have been a pupil of the Berlin Painter, the name vase of the PAINTER OF MUNICH 2413. The child Erichthonios, a founder king of Athens, is lifted by Mother Earth (Ge) into the arms of Athena, watched by a god and by Erotes poised on the tendrils by the vase handles. The god, probably Hephaistos, the donor father of the child (born from semen spilled on the earth after the god's attempted rape of Athena), is shown in the easy pose of what we recognise as the Early Classical in sculpture, as at Olympia, the weight of the body lightly shifted on to one leg but without the more emphatic leg crossing or primitive foreshortening of earlier artists. The pose is relaxed and plausible – as that of the Eros behind him – and rendered by light unfussy delineation of anatomy in paint which is unthinned but applied in light, sketchy but accurate strokes. Dress carries the sweeping hooks and broad loose folds which suit the heavier drapery and peplos-wearing figures of Early Classical – in sculpture too – and which represent the clearest break with Archaic pattern. The eyes are wide, lively, in good profile view, with straight upper lid, its top edge marked, but the pupil still mainly circular.

The Erichthonios vase was long considered the work of the artist HERMONAX but scholars, with Beazley's blessing, dissociate it now, and for all the similarities in style there is little enough in Hermonax to suggest that he was capable of this quality [*351–4*]. He signs four stamnoi, five pelikai and a cup. These, with neck amphorae, are his favourite shapes – not the big craters – and he decorates some smaller vases as well as a special line in ritual loutrophoroi with funeral or wedding scenes for home use only – graves and dedications on the Acropolis. Beazley saw him as a pupil of the Berlin Painter, and we can glimpse the mood of the master's cool figures especially on the Nolan amphorae, but not, unfortunately, his delicacy of touch although details are copied (e.g. ankle markings, lotus types). All the new details of Early Classical drawing are here – the hook folds, grouped lines on dress but with straight or at least not zigzag hems, open eyes. Floral friezes are becoming popular again, laurels [352] on pelikai and hydriai, and an occasional reversion to the older, straight-sided lotus type, and some looser tendrils. Apart from a range of ordinary komos and Dionysiac scenes, with a small range of myth, his speciality seems to be the Olympians, notably Zeus, together with an almost excessive fondness for pursuit scenes, secular or divine (Eos after Tithonos or Kephalos, Boreas and Oreithyia [352], Zeus and Aigina [351], Poseidon [353]). He was working from the late 470's probably to the mid century. The name vase of a follower, the PAINTER OF THE BIRTH OF ATHENA, presents a Pheidian theme, but the midget Athena bursting from Zeus' head is still Archaic [355]. His florals are atrocious, the figures little better.

The Berlin Painter decorated a number of Nolan amphorae and lekythoi throughout his career, notably later. These are popular shapes with minor Early Classical artists and a few may be mentioned here, especially the first, who is seen to be a pupil of the Berlin Painter. Beazley felt able to call the PROVIDENCE PAINTER an excellent artist [356–9]. After the Archaic we clearly have to look for other criteria of excellence, yet some – the precision, balance and pattern – are apparent still in the major Early Classical artists like the Niobid and Villa Giulia Painters, who are not considered in this book. The Providence Painter is neat and unpretentious, not oblivious to patterns of dress and body and reluctant to break with Archaic poses although details of dress and drawing, and some sobriety of mood, are in the new manner. Nolans and lekythoi offer no opportunity for elaborate scenes and only on some stamnoi and hydriai do we see groups of gods or minor myth. He likes pursuits of women, indeed most of his women seem in a hurry, carrying armour [358] or in domestic scenes – a bustle to which even his Athenas are not immune [357]. Details of drawing recall his master – eyes, earrings, ankles, some florals. He worked in the decades before and after 470 and praises Glaukon on several vases.

Other artists resemble him, and have the same interest in the beauty of Glaukon, and of Charmides, Nikon, Timoxenos and Hippon. They are lesser men, perhaps, in choice of subject-matter, and less prolific (the Providence Painter musters nearly a hundred and fifty attributions). The OIONOKLES PAINTER [360–3] displays some vigour and humour which can recall Skythes. The Dionysos and satyr [362] rehearse an old theme though in new dress, but the Persian ([360] fighting a Greek on the other side of the vase) reminds us of a new theme for vase painters inspired by recent encounters in the field; and the warrior cutting off a forelock [*361*], presumably for dedication, provides the opportunity for a display of armour which seems another of the painter's interests. The NIKON PAINTER [*364–6*] names Glaukon as kalos on the herm on [*364*], and adds his father's name Leagros, on another vase. He has bustling Athenas too, one with an aphlaston (ship's stern) celebrating a sea victory [*366*], no doubt the Battle of Salamis, and the vase will not be much later. Lekythoi in this group include some with white ground, not yet with funeral scenes. [*365*], probably by the Nikon Painter, shows the effect of the added colours (a 'second white' on the mistress' dress) on clothes and furniture, here quite well preserved. The CHARMIDES PAINTER offers satyrs at play [*367*], in what might be a skit on Aeneas' rescue of Anchises from Troy (compare [*135.1*]). It will have been observed that the ground line patterns on the Nolans of this series resemble those around cup tondos; and that some are short, some encircle the vase. The heyday for this whole group must be the 460's.

Cup painters

A few cup painters working mainly in the 460's continue in a weakened form the traditions of Late Archaic, not without some Mannerist flourishes. The academic tradition of Douris is recalled by several artists whose repertory rarely goes beyond the Dionysiac or the komos. I mention only the AKESTO-RIDES PAINTER [*368*]; THE EUAICHME PAINTER [*373*]; the DISH PAINTER [*371, 372*], who is a specialist in the stemmed dish shape, not cups; and the EUAION PAINTER [*369, 370, 374*], who is a prolific artist of some merit and more nearly Classical in mood although the ancestry of his small-headed, slim figures is clear enough. We are far from Archaic subtlety of composition in tondos now, and the Euaion Painter often introduces a high, sometimes patterned ground line for an upright two-figure group, and he likes the old elaborately patterned borders for tondos and the ground lines outside cups. On several cups by painters mentioned in this section we find lotuses swollen and simplified into knobbly ivy leaf shape, as well as the older variety with plump calyx and long centre leaf.

The following of Makron is naturally more robust, and this, combined with no little Mannerism, can make for humour. The CLINIC PAINTER [*376, 377*] is more than competent, perhaps more emphatic than his master in treatment of anatomy but a good observer. He is named for an aryballos in Paris showing surgery hour with 'cups' hanging on the wall, and a nice study of a dwarf [*377*]. The TELEPHOS PAINTER [*378–81*] is more mannered in the proportions of his figures and sometimes in his dress, but can be confident and imaginative in handling myth, not without what Beazley calls a 'smileless humour'. This is apparent in Eos' rapture seizing Tithonos in the Boston cup [*379*] where, outside, we have a thoroughly enigmatic scene of bewilderment and search conducted by older and young men, and a warrior silent below a peak. It has been associated with the story of the return to Athens of the descendants of Kephalos, whose name is that both of Eos' other sweetheart and of an Attic deme-hero. This is one of two of this painter's cups signed by Makron's potter, Hieron. On other vases Lichas is praised, a favourite of a full Classical artist, the Achilles Painter. The cup [380] presents an old theme but with a new use for flying drapery and notice the mannered florals, the racquet thyrsos.

Finally, the BOOT PAINTER, on whose cups Beazley wondered whether we see the latest work of the Kleophrades Painter. The figures undoubtedly have a certain stocky presence, but if they are his then the greatest of the Archaic artists had an interesting old age, brightened by these figures of naked Lolitas and their big boots [382]. The thematic change is intelligible, and where myth is shown it is handled with confidence; the stylistic change is admissible; this is the work of either a young man or second childhood.

350.1 Stamnos by the Painter of Munich 2413 (name vase). Birth of Erichthonios

350.2 Detail of 350.1

351 Stamnos by Hermonax.
Zeus and Aegina

352 Pelike signed by Hermonax.
Boreas and Oreithyia

353 Lekythos by Hermonax.
Poseidon and woman. H. 38

354 Stamnos by Hermonax. Death of Orpheus

355 Pelike by the Painter of the Birth of Athena (name vase)

357 Nolan amphora
by the Providence
Painter. Athena

358 Lekythos by the
Providence Painter

356 Lekythos by the Providence
Painter. H. 36·8

359 Nolan amphora
by the Providence
Painter. Dionysos in
gigantomachy

360 Nolan amphora by the Oionokles Painter. Persian. H. 33

361 Lekythos by the Oionokles Painter. H. 43·5

362 Nolan amphora by the Oionokles Painter. Dionysos and satyr

363 Nolan amphora by the Oionokles Painter. Herakles and Syleus

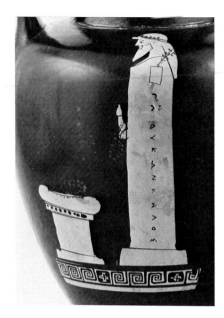

364 Nolan amphora by the Nikon Painter.
Herm

365 Lekythos by the Nikon
Painter. White ground. H. 42

367 Neck amphora by the Charmides Painter

366 Nolan amphora by the Nikon Painter.
Athena with aphlaston

368 *Cup by the Akestorides Painter.*
Hyakinthos

369 *Cup by the Euaion Painter. Atalanta*

370 *Cup by the Euaion Painter. Woman spinning*

371 Dish by the Dish Painter. Artemis

372 Dish by the Dish Painter

373 Cup by the Euaichme Painter

374 Cup by the Euaion Painter

375 Pyxis (Type A) by a follower of Douris. Hesperides. H. 14

376 Cup by the Clinic Painter. Herakles and Dionysos feast

377 Aryballos by the Clinic Painter (name vase). Clinic. H. 9

*378 Cup by the Telephos Painter (name vase).
Telephos at Argos*

379.1 Cup by the Telephos Painter. Eos and Tithonos

379.2 Outside of 379.1. Search party

380 Cup by the Telephos Painter

381 Cup by the Telephos Painter

382.1, 2 Cup by the Boot Painter

Chapter Five

SHAPES AND DATES

Shapes

The lengthy discussion in *ABFH* Chapter Nine obviates the necessity for detailed re-study of shapes, names and uses, and the development of many of the more important shapes has been considered in the course of the chapters on style. Some recapitulation and comment on new or complex shapes will suffice.

Amphorae. Of the belly amphorae very few of the old variety are still made beside the newer Type A with its angular handles and stepped foot [*8, 146, 171*]. Type C, with rolled lip and plain foot [*152*], has a limited vogue in Archaic red figure to about 450. Neck amphorae less often follow the standard late sixth-century scheme [*149, 164, 319*] but the small 'doubleens' with double-reeded handles and concave lips are made through the Late Archaic period [*164*]. There are Nikosthenic survivals [*56*], copies of the Panathenaic shape [*151, 162, 173, 307*] are particularly common after 500, and pointed versions resembling the plain wine jars [*132, 196*]. There are a few special varieties as well as different forms of handle – ridged, reeded, twisted [*138, 324*]. More important are the small, high-necked Nolan amphorae [*160, 360*], introduced about 490. Pelikai become very popular after 500, especially with the Mannerists [*142, 179, 180*, etc.]. Neck pelikai are rare [*383*].

Hydriai. The sixth-century shouldered type has a surprisingly long though tenuous existence to at least 480 [*175*]. One-piece kalpides are far commoner with the figure scene tending to spread off the shoulder and round on to the belly of the vase [*189*].

Oinochoai are easiest summarised by outlines of the varieties decorated in Archaic red figure, giving Beazley's classification (*see next page*). See also for Type 1 [*212*], Type 2 [*21*]. Type 3 is called a 'chous'; Type 8 are 'mugs'.

Craters and coolers. The column crater has a new lease of life in fifth-century red figure [*169, 170*], its handle plate supports now wholly columnar. The volute [*154, 181*] and calyx [*22, 24, 130, 188*, etc.] craters remain favoured for the most elaborate work. The former is often left with a black body; the latter's height comes to overtake its width in the 470's. The Syriskos Painter has a volute crater with figures on the handle sides, as there had been on the François

208

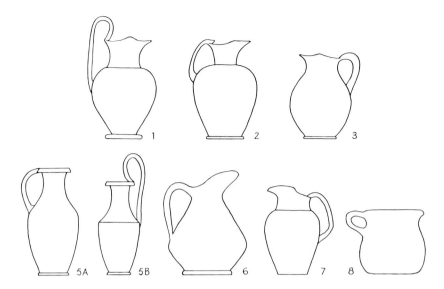

Vase. New is the bell crater which is represented on early red figure cups, but known in *corpore* only from about 500 on [*150*]. Some early examples are footless, and several have lugs [*335*] not loop handles which are later regular. Beazley thought the origin might lie in wooden vessels. We see the old dinos shape on [*32*]. The stamnos presents minor shape variations, tending to become slimmer as time passes [*32, 184, 198, 304, 351, 354*]. As well as the usual bulbous psykters [*58, 338*], some of which have ears (string holes for lids) we find one bucket-shaped cooler with a spout [*261*]. The ordinary psykter's life as a pottery shape is from the 520's to about 460.

Cups. The development of the principal varieties has been discussed already in the sections on Cup Painters. Pamphaios and Python make Chalcidising cups [*75*] for red figure (compare *ABFH* fig. *176*). Cup skyphoi, with shallow concave rims, resemble the common late black figure shape [*76, 206*] and there are later stemless cups with the flaring bowls of the stemmed variety. Skyphoi have tall, nearly straight walls (derived from the Corinthian kotyle of which there are one or two close imitations in red figure [*205, 309*]). A special type (B) is smaller, and its canonical form after 500 has one vertical, one horizontal handle. It is nowadays called a 'glaux' after the owl which commonly appears as its sole decoration later (the handles have also suggested to some a beak and tail). The kantharos, with upright handles, may have straight sides (Type A) or curving (Type C [*298*]), a red figure shape which may also be stemless (Type D), and is the variety favoured by Herakles. The kyathos dipper survives to the 480's [*234*], and is far rarer than in black figure.

Oil flasks. A few early lekythoi have the tapering or swelling profile of late black figure but later all are cylindrical in form [*210, 211, 249, 294*, etc.]. The squat lekythos appears by about 510 but only becomes really popular late in the fifth century. The spherical aryballos is still made [*282, 377*], as a refinement of the Corinthian shape (in use on [*4, 24.3*]), and the alabastron [*208, 209*], often white ground, recalling its original stone form. The askos is new, from the 480's on, with shallow (Shape 1) or deep (Shape 2) body, basket handle and oblique spout for careful pouring [*316*]. The shape recalls the wineskin with a tied orifice, whence its name (not applied to it in antiquity).

Ritual shapes. The lebes gamikos will become important again only later in red figure but the loutrophoros is decorated often after 500 with funeral scenes [*141*] or fights, occasionally with weddings. There are no exotic, decorated funerary shapes; no funerary plaques in red figure. Votive plaques are still made, however [*18, 52, 53*].

Other shapes. Lidded pyxides are commonest in their Type A form, with concave sides [*375*], or powder box (Type D) with slip-over lid. The plain cylindrical (Type B) and Nikosthenic [*97*] (early) are also seen. New are stemmed plates and dishes. Figure vases, usually in the form of human or animal heads with lips decorated in red figure, are made from about 500 on, and rhyta, copies of Eastern pouring vases with figure additions, from about 470; but the whole class, well represented later, is best considered elsewhere. Phintias made and signed some cockle-shell aryballoi, and there is the charming astragal [*204*], and odd sphinx stand [*103*]. Representations on vases suggest the existence of other, more fantastic shapes, often with phallic accessories [*284, 305*]: cf. *ABFH* fig. *177*.

Dates

The relative chronology of Archaic red figure depends on the clear stylistic development which can be traced, even within the work of a single artist, reinforced by criteria of shape and ornament. In such a closely studied field doubt may linger only over problems set by the length of time for which old styles or the working life of old-fashioned artists might continue, or over speculation about how early some innovations may have appeared. So a stylistic sequence may not be an absolute one but it is nearly so, and the warnings given about the chronology of black figure vases in *ABFH* p. 193 apply here too.

For absolute dating we can look for the same three types of evidence considered in *ABFH*:

(1) Vases or styles dated by events. Part of a Late Archaic cup tondo border in the Marathon tumulus (490) tells us no more than that the new border patterns are established by that date. Athens was sacked by the Persians in 480 and 479.

The stratification of the Acropolis debris is confused and confusing, although the concentration of Archaic vases should end about 479. In the Agora clearer deposits attributed to these years are found, but they are relatively poor in significant red figure pieces and do no more than confirm the suspected sequence. And since there is always the possibility that other occasions prompted the filling of some pits and wells, while 'Persian sack' debris can only be identified by the apparent date of its pottery, there is serious danger of circular argument. The destruction level at Eretria may well prove more informative, as well as further study of ostraka from Athens – potsherds with graffito names used in voting for ostracism. Their re-use for this purpose is sometimes dateable. For example, two fragments of vases by the Kleophrades Painter carry Megakles' name and so must have been painted, and broken, before Megakles was ostracised in 486 B C (though they might be from a possible second ostracism in the 470's). The evidence of kalos names we consider in Chapter Six (under Inscriptions) and symbolic use of myth at the start of Chapter Eight. A Pan Painter vase shows three herms, which may be those set up in the Agora to celebrate the capture of Eion in 476/475 B C. These complement rather than confirm the posited dating.

(2) Vases dated by their context with other objects for which a chronology has been established. There is no joy here, since there is no contemporary series of vases either prolific enough or well enough studied, as there had been earlier (the Corinthian series), and coins are no more closely dateable than vases.

(3) Vases or styles dated by stylistic comparisons with other objects for which a chronology has been established. The obvious comparisons are with sculpture. The reliefs of the Siphnian Treasury at Delphi, made little before 525, closely match the early Andokides Painter. The pedimental sculpture of the Temple of Apollo at Delphi, of about 510, is 'Pioneer'. The drapery of the Tyrannicides Group (477/476) has the looser folds of the latest Archaic drawing.

Chapter Six

GENERAL DECORATION

Chapters Eleven to Thirteen in *ABFH* cover much that is relevant also to any discussion of the decoration of red figure vases, and in the corresponding chapters of this volume I shall avoid much repetition except in the interest of pointing out differences, changes or innovations. It will be understood that by red figure I refer to the Archaic period covered in this book. There is a significant later development of figures and scenes, both genre and myth.

Conventions

Iconographic conventions were never more stereotyped in Greek art than in Athenian black figure. Many persist in red figure, but a characteristic of the new technique is the freedom of composition which it offers. This has a striking effect on the arrangement of stock scenes and promotes a multiplicity of new ones, but a number of newly mastered poses themselves acquire a degree of canonisation and can be taken as hallmarks of the Archaic red figure style in its various phases – for instance the frontal-with-profile legs, crossed legs, poses designed to exhibit growing command of foreshortening. After the Archaic period new inspiration is drawn from major painting, not considered here.

The more realistic gestures of red figure mean that we have often to turn to latter-day experience of the theatre or our more theatrical contemporaries for explanation. Facial expression remains limited although much more is managed by pose and gesture. Frontal and the rare three-quarter faces are not reserved wholly for grotesques like centaurs [39.2, 139, 268], satyrs [132.2], wine bibbers [25, 27, 51.1], pipers [35] or helmeted heads [114, 337.2], and become used more often to invite the viewer's sympathy [381] or attention – victims [3.1, 135.2, 277], Nikai [348], the preoccupied [18, 262.2], etc. [227.2]. Definition of age by head and pose is much improved, thinned paint as well as white being used to indicate greying hair. The artist is more aware of live forms and poses but not yet prepared to forego the pattern conventions of his figures in the interests of mere realism.

Inscriptions

Inscriptions are painted in red, rarely white or incised, on the black background. They have often lost their colour and then can only be traced by catching the dulled surface in reflected light. The red figure artist was as arbitrary as the black figure artist had been in his use of them. The best are often silent about their identity, the poorest vociferous, but we have more red figure names than black figure and a fair range of potter signatures. Nonsense inscriptions are rarer after the early fifth century. General captions, such as were seen occasionally in black figure, are not found, but legends issuing from the figures' mouths are more popular and the Pioneers' vases are sometimes quite noisy. Conversations are rarities, however: 'Look, a swallow', 'Yes, by Herakles', 'There it is; it's spring already' – on a Pioneer vase close to Euphronios. Bespoke inscriptions, as for dedications, are almost unknown, and mercantile graffiti far fewer than in the later sixth century.

Kalos inscriptions praising the beauty of contemporary youths remain popular, with or without the proper names, or affirmatives (karta, naichi). The significance and the dating value of the kalos names was discussed in *ABFH* p. 201. In red figure more can be plausibly identified with Athenians otherwise known, but still few are chronologically useful. I mention some of the more interesting, naming their painter-admirers in brackets. Leagros, favourite of some black figure artists and the Pioneers (Euphronios, Euthymides, Thalia Painter, Kiss Painter, Eleusis Painter, Proto-Panaitian and Onesimos, Colmar Painter), was a contemporary of Themistokles (born about 524) and plausibly kalos about 510–500. His son Glaukon, born about 490 and a general in 441/440, was kalos about 475–465. The Hipparchos (Epiktetos) is probably not the tyrant but husband of his niece. Megakles (Phintias, Euthymides) had a most probably younger sister born, it seems, about 520–510, and was himself ostracised in 486. Miltiades, the Marathon victor, and his brother Stesagoras must have been born before 550 and were a little old to be praised in early red figure (Paseas and near the Salting Painter respectively). Oltos' long allegiance to Memnon might seem to call into question the short period in which we assume a youth remained popularly kalos, but Oltos may be deliberately reacting against the usual practice and praising the hero Memnon, slain at Troy and marked out as handsome by the poets. On a contemporary vase showing Memnon's duel he is called 'kalos', so the idea was familiar.

Letter shapes are now uninformative. Ionic forms and spellings of the type familiar to us from modern printing (of capitals) become increasingly common with the fifth century and the letters square up more, losing their Archaic slanting forms.

Florals and Ornament

Late black figure florals and other border patterns appear still on early red figure, becoming less common with the start of the fifth century except on shapes more commonly associated with the old technique such as amphorae of Panathenaic form, lekythoi or column craters. Red figure palmette friezes, the flowers circumscribed and separate or in scrolls, or in the fifth century set in oblique pairs, are used for rim and border patterns on the finer vases, or in ones or grouped by many cup handles. Generally this ornament gets more sparse in the early fifth century, reviving in the second quarter when the laurel wreath, a common rim pattern in later red figure, begins to make a regular appearance. From about 520 a new lotus type is attached to palmette scrolls, with squat springy sepals and a long centre leaf with various palmette leaves filling. Not all painters use these flowers and they help define hands, as we have seen. With the second quarter of the fifth century there is a reversion to the older lotus type with straight stiff petals, often combined in a frieze with palmettes in the old manner. On few red figure vases are the florals of much importance in the design, but there are some with florals only, notably the Group of the Floral Nolans.

The squat lotus was derived from East Greek florals in the form with which Attic black figure painters had also experimented. From the same source come the maeanders which include pattern squares used to border cup tondos and as base lines from about 500 on, and which had been used sporadically in Athenian black figure (Antimenes Painter). Note how some maeander patterns can be 'read' in a reserving, red figure manner. The only other important red figure pattern is the ovolo of short tongues, for base lines or lips. Rays at the bases of the larger vases become very rare in the fifth century.

Animals and Monsters

Animals virtually cease to serve as major elements of decoration in red figure. The occasional black vase – lekythos, hydria or stamnos – has a small animal device with or without florals, and isolated animals may be stationed beneath handles on other shapes. Silhouette animal friezes appear still on shapes with a strong black figure past, notably on lips or necks of some column craters. Shield blazons, usually animal, are also silhouette as a rule, rarely red figure [26]. We may single out the fine black crows on many shields, about and after 500, and good lions, some outline drawn on early vases. The lion regularly adopts the crouching, bottom-in-air, one-paw-raised pose, with small head and bristling mane, very different from the creatures of animal-frieze black figure.

Special scenes with animals include several with horses – being groomed and combed [229], or with their masters [228] and being inspected at the annual dokimasia. Pets are prominent. The hare and cock had appeared long before as love gifts [373] but there are explicit scenes of cock fighting now, and the way some hares are being set down suggests coursing [48.3]. Dogs are still common, with men, and water birds, with women, while martens, foxes ([64] cf. [210]) and a panther-cub [117] make their appearance with men, and the fox alone stealing grapes (a shield device by Skythes). The boar [240] and deer [237] are hunted (rare hitherto on vases). There are far fewer of the flying birds, space filling or as omens. On the whole, the best animal studies, apart from the horses or sacrificial bulls [8, 211], are called for by myth scenes – the lions, bulls and deer fought for or with by heroes. The camel with a negro boy [183] is exceptional.

The monsters too fall from favour as independent motifs, but sphinxes, winged horses and griffins stand by the handles of some early cups [62, 93]. The griffin loses his Archaic forehead knob and, after 500, acquires a spiny mane. The cock-horse is still ridden on early red figure, and once the cock alone [cover]. The dolphins ridden on [58] may refer to some mummery. Winged dolphins recall the many mixed monsters of East Greek art and probably are inspired by them, but they are rare, since the tendency is to expunge the monstrous and exotic.

383 Neck pelike by the Berlin Painter. H. 33

Chapter Seven

SCENES OF REALITY

Observation of live forms was still sporadic and did not yet lead to full understanding of how they function, but it did enhance the new freedom of drawing and may have contributed to freer use of everyday and genre subjects on vases. Interest in the behaviour of his fellow men and women was no novelty for a Greek artist – think of Homer – and I doubt whether Athens' new democracy can claim much credit for the vase painter's wider repertory since a similar freedom is apparent in his use of myth. A result is the creation of new stock scenes, but also a loosening of the older iconographic conventions.

Everyday life

Everyday dress in red figure is as it has been described for black figure (*ABFH* pp. 205–6) but the new technique admits more detail of all but surface patterning (except early). Women are more elaborately dressed now. The chiton is still preferred, but the peplos becomes increasingly common and details of the pin or brooch fastening at the shoulders, over bare arms, may be shown. The hair may be bound in a cloth (sakkos) sometimes with a tail hanging free behind and in early red figure the forehead and temple ringlets rival those of the marble korai. Otherwise fillets or diadems are worn and occasionally a small loose scarf [*294*]. There are far more details of jewellery – earrings, armlets and bracelets, anklets (one leg only as a rule), but not finger rings. Notice the seals or amulets tied on to the limbs or round the necks of naked women [*27*] and (later) children. A bra helps those who lead an active life (Atalanta [*369*] and [*346*]). In men's dress, we may notice towards the end of our period the hunter's boots, with heavy transverse stripes for the lacing rather than the stiffer tongued variety of earlier days or the soft boots with lappets. These are often worn with chlamys (short cloak) and petasos (brimmed hat) and, with two spears, identify a hunter [*347*]. Beards and moustaches may be worn, not moustaches alone, and the hair of younger men is more often shown cropped in the fifth century. Naked, both sexes show all their body hair, except under arm, but there is the odd scene of a woman singeing off her pubic hair, and a loving couple are once threatened by a lamp in that quarter. Foreskins are very rarely withdrawn, even on erections. Tattooing on necks,

216

arms and legs, is reserved for Thracian women – nurses or killing Orpheus [277]. Red figure naturally presents more problems than black figure when it comes to depicting negroes (except in outline [208]), but there seem to be other real attempts to distinguish foreigners [126, 336], and the anatomy of a dwarf is properly observed: [258] for pygmies, and [377].

The fountain house scenes, as in black figure, appear in red figure [44] seldom after about 500, but there are some showing group bathing (not mixed [4]). Private ablution becomes a very common subject, especially in the early fifth century, with a standed laver and generally no more than one girl or youth beside it [109], and there are many bathing scenes with women busy with their clothes [224], or with boots [382] and sandals. The painters are displaying an early (for Greek art) interest in the female nude, but are slow to render essential features plausibly, as we have noted. A number of scenes have women spinning or working wool [267, 293, 370], especially after 500. The wool basket (kalathos) with splaying sides is a regular piece of furniture.

Domestic entertainment is demonstrated by boys with hoops [236] (as also Ganymede), bird cages [51.2, 244] and toy chariots which have leaf sails [318]; and there are girls on a see-saw [322]. Architecture, domestic or otherwise, is even more summary than in black figure, with at the most a token column and strip of Doric entablature [274]. There are several school scenes with lessons in pipes, lyre [38, 328] and reading from scrolls [234, 289], with equipment, including writing tablets, hanging on the wall behind. The clinic on [377] is exceptional.

Fighting

Red figure is no less explicit about armour than black figure had been. The vulnerable high-crested helmets are seen less often [2] but there are still some half crests [114] and transverse. The standard helmet types are the Corinthian (as *Frontispiece* and often), Chalcidian with rounded cheek pieces [49, 53, 79], and Attic [3.2, 43, 50.1, 135.2] with hinged cheek pieces, to which is added the Thracian which has a more pointed crown, often with a peak and elaborate cheek pieces [315]. Decorated helmets appear, sometimes with relief ornament over the forehead – hair ringlets [285.2], snakes, leaves as of a crown (compare Athena on coins) – but fewer with the horns or feathers we saw in black figure.

The linen corselet, with shoulder pieces tied across the chest and worn over a short chiton [33.1, 281], soon wholly replaces the rigid bell corselet, and an innovation of the fifth century is the modelled body corselet [361]. An unusual garment is a skirt of heavy material [266, 361] sometimes worn without a corselet. There are the usual greaves which may be shown with their stand in arming scenes [140, 262.1] and are worn padded at the ankles [*Frontispiece*], but only early examples of the thigh- and arm-guards seen in black figure [2].

Apart from the hoplite shield and its Boeotian variant [2.2 right, 285.2], believed heroic, we see the crescent-shaped pelta in the hands of light-armed troops, some Amazons, Persians [360], even satyrs [31, 66]. The kopis or machaira cutlass with curving blade is rather commoner now [186], besides the usual straight sword. In contemporary hoplite practice the thrusting spear is the basic weapon. Not only Amazons may carry a battle axe [129.1, 360].

The Thracian patterned cloak (zeira) is seen, especially for horsemen [26], and the Thracian fox-skin cap (alopekis) or its equivalent in dappled hide [228], worn in Athens as fashionable or appropriate riding gear. Other soft caps are the high-crowned or pointed Scythian [12, 13, 17, 45, 77, etc.], worn still with the usual Oriental patterned costume of archers and Amazons, but also a more closely fitting version, and the type with a looser crown which is worn by Persians [303.1].

The commonest warrior scenes remain the arming [86, 93, 281, etc.] and the departure from home [45], sometimes with a libation poured or entrails inspected for omens [129.1]. Besides the usual fighting scenes there are some of warriors crouching in ambush [167]. Archers test their arrows by looking along them to see that they are straight [12], and some string their bows, bending them across their thighs. Long hair has to be rolled up on a knife or sword to tuck into a helmet (cf. [281]), but the cutting of locks is also seen, no doubt for dedication [331, 361]. Trumpets are blown, angled down for testing [43], up for summons [66], and a conch [93]. Fewer chariots appear, except in myth scenes. It is doubtful whether they had any warlike application in Greece at this date. Real cavalry is to be distinguished from the mounted hoplites accompanied by squires. More warrior dances (pyrrhic) are shown in red figure, accompanied on the pipes [127].

Entertainment, public and private

Recitals, with the soloists standing on a low platform (bema), are shown in black figure [138], but in these early years of the history of the theatre in Greece it is harder to identify stage scenes or players, although the popularity of some myth subjects might already owe something to their treatment by playwrights, as before by poets. The satyr play undoubtedly attracts the artist since imitation of his favourite humanoid is involved, and we shall return to this subject, but there are more scenes of satyr play, dithyramb or dramatic choruses on later vases [333]. There are a few red figure additions to the black figure scenes of pantomime, like the dolphin riders [58].

The symposion drinking party receives its classic expression in Archaic red figure. The setting may be outdoor, moving from house to house with cups, pipes and girls, or the dining-room (andron) with couches, one occasionally seen end on [290] since they are set along the walls of small rectangular rooms, on which can hang lyres, baskets, pipe cases. The three-legged side tables with food on them are sometimes omitted now but we see some basins for foot washing, opportunely placed for other purposes, and lampstands [112].

The men wear little or nothing, and in the fifth century take to thick or padded fillets for their hair, like sweat bands. Naked boys fill their cups, carrying ladle and sieve for the service [248 right]. Girls may do this too but more often play pipes or sit on the couches to entertain the men. They rarely strip [46, 129.2, 265], and girl pipers usually have ungirt chitons. Yet nakedness, but for headdress and amulets, is admitted for the all-women parties seen in early red figure: [27, 38] cf. [225]. Incidental and related scenes include several of youths with vats or craters, presumably cleaning them in preparation for the feast.

Entertainment is varied and usually supplied by the party-goers who play, sing or attempt balancing tricks with their cups [68] or while riding wineskins [105]. The game of kottabos is played by spinning a cup from the finger and directing the dregs of wine at a target in mid floor. The gesture [38, 305], but not the target, is shown often in this period and may be accompanied by a toast. Professional entertainment, apart from music, is provided by acrobats and perhaps by the pyrrhic war dances performed mainly later by near-naked girls. Men now are to be seen playing clappers (krotala) [108, 255], hitherto a girl's instrument [6, 11]. The pipes case, with side pocket for the mouthpiece, is a common feature, as on [21, 46, 51.1, 78]. The painters do not shrink from describing the excretory or nauseous relief a body seeks after too much wine [84, 254].

Elderly komasts wearing chitons [178, 334], mitra-turbans over their hair, and sometimes carrying parasols, appear in some scenes from about 520 on. On a Kleophrades Painter vase with such figures [131] one holds a lyre labelled Anakreon, the Ionian poet who came to Athens in about 520 and who may have introduced this drag performance which remained fashionable for over fifty years. The headdress was suitable for men in Lydia but could only have been regarded as effeminate in Athens. Anakreon's poetic view of the good time (euphrosyne) is very much that of the red figure symposion. He died in Athens soon after Marathon, aged eight-five, choked by a grape pip, they said.

The many and varied scenes of sexual activity, although no doubt promoted by a drinking party, are rarely shown in a specific symposion setting although beds sometimes are used. There is no fuller record of man the lover in any other medium or period of Greek art; few to rival it in the history of art, outside Japan. The courting scenes of black figure continue [51.2, 214, 226, 260], but more are heterosexual now [214, 222] and the chaster kiss and cuddle are not neglected [123]. All the basic positions of love-making are shown [46, 99, 112, 219, 302, 346] with no special preference, now that cushions or furnishings have rendered obsolete the advantages of the standing entry from behind, favoured earlier, as [18, 272, 297]. Aids may be clothes hanging from the wall [233], and either partner may wield a slipper to add piquancy: [112, 233, 241] and cf. [30]. Note the inscribed injunction on [297] to 'keep still', and the splendidly irrelevant praise of a handsome youth on [219]. Male masturbation is shown, and once even female [112]. The Greek wine amphora with its narrow cylindrical neck and pointed toe is an unexpected aid for both men (at least, satyrs [73]) and women (squatting on the upturned jar). Homosexual activity is exclusively male and heterosexually sucking is more in order than licking [99]. This is a man's world.

Model phalloi are often shown, even a two-ended one [99]. Some are simple dildos, and so used [71]: others are larger and may be carried by women or kept in baskets [176, 342]. The knob is often decorated with an eye, as other objects (ships) which have to find their way. It would be easier to believe that these objects were being used for some religious, fertility purpose, if they were ever in the hands of other than naked women or satyrs. With the phallos-headed bird [176] we are taken into the realm of psychology rather than myth. They appear handled by women, ridden by a satyr, even as shield blazons.

Sport

The nakedness of youths exercising at the palaistra could well have been an important source of inspiration for the Greek artist who was becoming increasingly aware of the possibilities of representing the physiology of subtle balance and movement in painting and sculpture. Athlete figures on vases or in marble from now on serve as demonstrations of this new skill. The range of sports shown on vases remains the same as in the sixth century, but an infinitely greater variety of poses are chosen for depiction in any one event or act, such as throwing the discus. Of particular events in red figure we may pick out the growing popularity of races for armed men – the hoplitodromoi [79, 82, 230]. The event was introduced at Olympia in 520 and seems not to appear any earlier on Athenian vases. The pankration (all-in wrestling) is shown with some detailing of holds, legitimate and otherwise [263]. The picks (sometimes only one-pronged) shown in some scenes are for loosening the ground for the long jump [227.1], an event in which the athlete is assisted by hand weights (halteres) [85.2, 286].

Trainers carry long staffs or canes [3, 97], and sometimes use them. They may make notes or record wins on tablets: [235] cf. [307]. The athletes are naked but may wear exercise caps [227, 369]. The oil bottle, sponge and strigil (for scraping down) is regular equipment seen hanging [51.2, 230, 260] or being carried by a child attendant [239, 259]. The thick oil is being shaken out into the hand on [4, 24.3]. Some men practise infibulation, tying up the foreskin with a cord for modesty, protection or to discourage the distraction of an erection [24.1 left, 230]. Athletes provide the largest single class of everyday life scenes in Archaic red figure.

Commerce and industry

The most informative workshop scenes show artists – potters and painters at the wheel [101], with brushes, or moving to the kiln; metalsmiths [101, cf. 174] (and more probably so than potters on the Caputi hydria [323]); sculptors in bronze [262], marble [264], wood [74]; carpenters [124, cf. 192]; armourers, especially with helmets [81, 262]. The presence of Athena in some of these scenes [101, 264, 323] is a delicate self-compliment by the artist, and reflection of her function as Ergane.

We see far less of the retail trade – no weighing scenes now and only one or two butchers in early red figure, or some later perfumiers on pelikai. The countryside is mainly ignored, with a few yokels riding a goat [180] or ram, chased by Pan [335.1], and men fishing [119, 344] (and recall Paris, when shown with his flocks on Ida before the Judgement [310]). For an occasional vintage scene we turn to satyrs. There are no more important ship scenes, except in the service of myth (Odysseus and the Sirens). In general the scenes to be noted under this head show a markedly metropolitan and artistic interest, rather narrower than the repertory in black figure.

Religion

The commonest scenes are extremely simple with just one or two men or women by an altar. Worship at herms is shown fairly often, and sometimes we see small votive plaques hanging in the field as from a tree [278, 364, cf. 330], as also hanging by the furnace on [262], with masks. On [340] meat is cooked on a spit over the altar where the bones and fat burn and a libation is poured. There are a few more elaborate scenes of procession to an altar, with sacrificial animals and the distinctive openwork baskets being carried [211]. The altars commonly have volute tops, and the regular red marks at the sides are thought to be wipings from the blood of victims: as [245.2, 330]. In myth scenes we see an occasional cult statue [135.1] or tripod [245.2]. A mask of Dionysos on a dressed pillar may be the centrepiece for a vinous festival involving maenad impersonation by dancing priestesses [311], and apparently wine tasting. A special act is the entrail inspection as a warrior departs [129.1], and there are many scenes of libation, pouring into and from a phiale or cup, for arrivals and departures, often beside altars and even by gods.

Funeral plaques are not made in red figure and prothesis (the laying out of the body) is seen only on some ritual loutrophoroi [141]. Votive plaques in red figure of this date are few – found only on and near the Acropolis. They are often of high merit and show Athena [52], gods, myth, even erotic scenes [18]. The chariot marriage processions of black figure disappear.

Historical figures

The vase painters were as quick to put Persians fighting Greeks on their vases [*279, 303, 360*] as Aeschylus was to put Persians on the stage after the Persian Wars. The dead of Marathon were treated as heroes, and near contemporaries or recent events had to have a heroic status before Greeks would admit them in their art, at least at this date. Which is why the 'transvestite' figures are Anakreontic rather than Anakreon himself (see above). Sappho and Alcaeus [*261*] were long enough dead (over fifty years) and well enough honoured to qualify (and see *ABFH* fig. *311*). The murder of Hipparchos (514 BC) had brought heroisation and the honour of a statuary group to his slayers [*199*] and might be tacitly equated with the execution of Aigisthos. Croesus' defeat and the story of his escape from the pyre (546 BC) had already receded into myth history [*171*]. The naming of contemporaries in symposia was naturally exempt from restrictions observed in more formal scenes or senior arts.

Chapter Eight

SCENES OF MYTH

The scenes of myth on early red figure vases are affected by the same new conditions and possibilities offered by the new technique as were the genre scenes. Stock iconographic conventions for episodes are soon broken, or considerably diversified in the interests of telling more of a story. Many new subjects are introduced but it is still possible to present the familiar scenes in excerpt only and to make full use of allusive detail. Even so we are far from having a full pictorial statement of many stories or even a canonical one in terms of stories most fully known to us from other sources. An historical approach to the development of myth in art is as important as it is in literature.

The source of the new scenes or cycles is to be sought largely in the artists' own reactions to the new conditions offered them. We may suspect more intellectuals in their number now, more literate. For the first time it becomes clear that poems, new or old, are inspiring the choice of new scenes, notable being the interest in Troy in the early fifth century. The narration of myth on the Athenian stage, and the importance of the new mural compositions in sanctuaries and public buildings also played their part in influencing both themes and figures, but their effect is mainly later. Aeschylus is a Late Archaic artist too, but it is easier to recognise the influence of the novel themes of Aeschylus' satyr plays [163, 325] than any special versions of epic stories from his tragedies, and not often possible to identify accurately in earlier poets, other than Homer, versions which vase painters deliberately followed.

One or two general iconographic trends may be noted before we turn to details (supplementing the account in *ABFH* Chapter Thirteen rather than repeating it). One is the rejection of the monstrous: Gorgons soon humanise and there are far fewer hero-versus-monster duels although the decorative or symbolic value of sphinxes is not forgotten, nor of course the utterly plausible centaurs and satyrs, the latter being at their most vigorous in these years. Another tendency is to render deities and heroes more youthful, beardless, this applying at different rates to almost all except the acknowledged seniors like Zeus, Poseidon, Hephaistos, or father-figures like Nereus and Priam. At Troy most heroes remain bearded except Achilles and, sometimes, Patroklos.

The symbolic or allusive use of myth to comment on events of the day, or deliberate political promotion of myth remain hard to detect. If Herakles was

223

the hero of Peisistratan Athens, then Theseus is of the new democracy. This is demonstrated clearly enough on vases and elsewhere, culminating in Kimon's recovery of Theseus' bones for Athens. After Marathon there is a great spate of Nike figures on vases which surely allude to the victory: not directly because the context is very rarely military rather than religious, musical, athletic or vague, but military success may have promoted a new interest in her cult and special association with Athena, and so greater attention to her function in other contests. At Artemisium in 480 the Persian fleet was scattered and defeated by the North Wind, as it had been twelve years earlier off Athos, and accordingly the Athenians honoured Boreas and built him a temple. It has been suggested that this provoked the new interest in scenes showing Boreas abducting Oreithyia, who was an Attic princess. The artists who introduced the scenes are so obsessed by other scenes of pursuit (Eos with her young men; Zeus, Poseidon, Theseus with various girls) that we should be cautious in attributing special importance to Boreas. From about 470 on the girl chased by Zeus on vases is sometimes identified as Aigina, whose island distinguished itself at Salamis in 480, but was the bane of Athens before and after, suffering defeat in 459. But is it Aigina on the earlier vases, and did anything political or military popularise this otherwise unimportant story? Speculation in this subject is hazardous.

It should be remarked that the apparent popularity of some stories in red figure only after about 500 must in part be due to the restricted production and shapes in red figure before that date.

The Gods

In red figure, especially after 500, the Olympians are seen more often in independent studies or involved in stories peculiar to them rather than to any protégé. Particularly common are libation scenes where deities alone pour from a phiale, or are served by others (Zeus with Iris or Nike, Apollo with Artemis, Athena with Herakles, etc.) in the ritual of greeting or departure [193, 202].

ZEUS is a far commoner figure now, often in quiet groups with other deities, as [55.1]. The *Birth of Athena* fully armed from his head is still for long shown in the older scheme, with the diminutive and precocious figure emergent [355], but soon to be shown full-grown beside her sire, as on the Parthenon, though it is a less common subject than in black figure. New are repeated scenes of Zeus' pursuit of a woman and of *Ganymede* [150, 339], shown as a youth, often with hoop and stick and holding a cock (a pet or love gift). On the identity of the woman as *Aigina* [351], see above; but *Thetis* is also chased, a match averted since her son was fated to be stronger than his father. *Europa* with the Zeus bull [147] is particularly popular in the first quarter of the fifth century.

APOLLO appears as another womaniser but he is most commonly shown as a musician [*197*], and often with his sister. The Berlin Painter gives him a winged tripod for his journey overseas [*157*]. He still has to deal with *Tityos*, who attacked their mother Leto [*41.1*]. On a few vases Apollo challenges Idas for *Marpessa*, who preferred the hero to the god. The girl's father Euenos intervenes on the Pan Painter's version [*338*], while from the other side of the vase Zeus sends Hermes to intercede. A boy riding a swan [*368*] on some early red figure is usually taken for *Hyakinthos*, Apollo's favourite, whom he allowed to ride his swan chariot.

HERMES, ubiquitous in scenes where others take the leading roles, has still himself to dispatch *Argos*, set by Hera to guard Io, the cow [*165, 327*]. Argos has a body full of eyes now rather than two heads as in black figure. Hermes' infant escapade, stealing *Apollo's cattle*, is shown by the Brygos Painter, the child-god bestowed in a winnowing basket [*251*]; and he is seen as an adult with cattle, playing a lyre [*96*].

DIONYSOS' popularity hardly needs dwelling upon. He is commonly with his rout of satyrs and maenads, often with his consort Ariadne, but he reclines in a more civilised symposion also, sometimes with other gods including the promoted Herakles [*376*]. His processional *Return of Hephaistos* to Olympus remains an important theme [*130, 295.2*]. Makron shows him as a child carried by Zeus to his nymph nurses. A Dionysiac subject reserved for red figure is the rending limb from limb of king *Pentheus* by his mother and her frenzied companions [*28*], a story best known to us from Euripides' *Bacchae*. Another tale, but without text authority, is of the satyrs' *assault on Hera* and Iris, as depicted by the Brygos Painter [*252*]. There is an uncertain black figure attack on Hera, but elsewhere Iris pays the penalty of wayfarers and is attacked again, but by centaurs [*139*], so we may doubt whether there was any canonic literary version and may regard this as a logical extension of satyric behaviour towards maenads.

HEPHAISTOS' lameness is not emphasised by the fifth century, but he is once or twice given a winged chariot [*120*], probably one of his own marvellous inventions. Otherwise he wears short working dress and carries tongs or a wood axe. The satyrs in his forge suggest a satyr play [*174*].

POSEIDON's consort may be Aithra (who bore him Theseus in one version of his story) or Amphitrite. Trident and fish identify him [*59*], while both Amphitrite and the sea nymphs who attend them may hold fish. *Amymone*, rescued by him from a satyr at a fountain or well, was then seduced by him and from the 460's he is seen chasing her on vases. Other women he pursues are anonymous [*353*]. ARES remains a nonentity.

ATHENA is naturally the most popular goddess. On her aegis-bib the gorgoneion is now more regularly shown, as [*3.2*]. We have noted her birth from Zeus' head. Otherwise she is mainly engaged supporting heroes or on civic tasks – escorting or entertaining her protégé Herakles [*146, 188*]; in settings recalling her role as goddess of the Panathenaia and its games [*307*]; with Nike, and holding an aphlaston (ship's stern) to celebrate a victory, presumably Salamis or Artemisium [*249, 366*]; attending the workshops of her citizens, and the birth of *Erichthonios* [*329, 350*], the Athenian hero and her foster-child, handed over by Earth (Ge). The last appears only after the Persian Wars when Athena seems to become respected more for her own sake as city goddess than for her patronage of heroes.

The vulnerability of Hera and Iris to the sub-human has been noted above. HERA is shown in various Olympian gatherings, distinguished by sceptre and crown. IRIS, winged, is the counterpart to Hermes and may carry a herald's caduceus, but often simply attends Zeus or pours libations for him [*202*]. She is readily confused with Nike except where the latter is clearly celebrating victory – with phiale, often by an altar [*213*] or incense burner [*159*]; carrying a tripod or hydria prize, lyre [*348*] or wreath [*161*].

DEMETER and her daughter carry torches or ears of corn and wear low crowns, but they usually appear only to dispatch *Triptolemos* in his mission to bring agriculture to earth [*154, 189, 309*]. His wheeled throne is now usually powered by winged snakes.

APHRODITE [*55.2*] enjoys no special scenes but makes a good show at the Judgement of Paris [*310*]. EROS, or a multiplicity of Erotes (Himeros and others [*184*]), becomes suddenly popular from the 490's, usually in single studies [*173, 204, 316*], carrying a lyre or hare, or pursuing a boy; and he serves in myth [*294, 308, 310*]. ARTEMIS supervises the killing of *Aktaion* by his dogs [*335.2, 337.1*]. Only later is the hunter's transformation into a stag indicated by added horns. She is more the archer-huntress now, but her primitive form as a winged Goddess of Animals is not entirely forgotten [*212*].

PAN started as all-goat. In the fifth century his body and limbs are mainly human, but despite the favour he found in Athens after his help at Marathon, he is not much shown in the first half of the fifth century [*335.1*].

The gods sit or stand together often still, either in council on Olympus or observing – the birth of Athena, the arrival of Dionysos. Their action together, fighting the *Giants*, follows the schemes established in black figure, often with more explicit or novel detail [*187, 196, 280, 337*]. Thus, Hephaistos now hurls his burning coals at the foe, and Dionysos' vine is seen trapping a giant [*280.2*]; in black figure Hephaistos is heating the coals and Dionysos is assisted only by animals. Poseidon's island missile may be tricked out with appropriate wild life.

Herakles

The hero who dominated the myth repertory of Athenian black figure had a reduced role on the later vases. Various factors are responsible for this – a growing aversion from the monstrous; a growing preference for the new

226

democracy's hero, Theseus, over the tyrants' hero; and in the period when the still-flourishing black figure and the new red figure overlap, the progressive artists are quicker to take up the new trends, so that it is only in earliest red figure that the black figure mood is maintained. But there are several new scenes involving the hero to entertain us.

We take the canonic Labours first. The encounters with the *Lion* [7, 10, 104] and with *Amazons* [9, 29, 149, 298] retain much of their appeal throughout our period. The delivery of the *Boar* to terrified Eurystheus [89], the fight with *Geryon* [26.2], with the *Hydra* [198], with the *Bull*, the removal of *Kerberos* from Hades [16], and the visit to the *Hesperides* and Atlas, are not wholly forgotten, and there are examples with as much or more explicit detail than before. The rest are virtually ignored. Some interest, however, is maintained in subsidiary episodes. We see Herakles in his *Golden Bowl* [300], provided by the Sun; the wrestling with *Nereus* [156] to discover the route west, with Nereus wholly human now (one exception) and exhibiting only slight mutations, but quite often accompanied by his daughters or even Triton (the fight with the fishy Triton has disappeared); the drinking party with centaur *Pholos* beside the open wine pithos, and the resultant fight with the *centaurs* [72].

Some but not all of the other popular black figure episodes recur with the same formula: the match with the giant *Antaios* whom Euphronios gives realistically barbarian features [23]; the attack on the sleeping giant *Alkyoneus* [42, 95], with Sleep (Hypnos) perched upon him; rarely, the *Kerkopes* bagged [181]; the reception of King *Eurytos* and slaying of his perfidious sons [231]; the fight with *Kyknos* [65] but now without Zeus intervening between Herakles and Ares, or at most his thunderbolt; and the best of the fights with the Egyptian King *Busiris* [75, 336] and his followers at the altar where they intended to sacrifice Herakles, which offer interesting studies of the artists' developing views on the physiognomy and anatomy of Africans.

To win his bride Deianira Herakles fought the river god *Acheloos*. Oltos is unique in showing him with a fishy body [54], rather than bovine, but the scene remains rare otherwise – monstrous, as does the slaying of *Nessos* who tried to rape the girl [121]. The quarrel with *Apollo* over the tripod [40.1, 94] has a remarkable run of popularity just through our period but not later, and we should perhaps look for some special symbolism which sustained it in these years. The complementary dispute over the deer is still rare.

Athena's special role as Herakles' patron naturally remains important. It had been so long before and outside Athens. They appear often together, in conversation, with libations, in action. But his *Introduction to Olympus* [50.2] by her, especially by chariot, falls from favour, understandably if it had some tyrant symbolism and despite its propriety as part of the hero's story.

The new Herakles scenes involve his childhood, one or two trivial adventures, and possibly reflect stage themes. Some appear also in contemporary

227

late black figure. The Berlin Painter is the first to show him wrestling with the *snakes* sent by the ever unfriendly Hera while he was still in his cradle [*155*]. He reacted predictably badly to school and killed his music teacher *Linos* with his lyre [*296*]. He receives his baby son Hyllos from his wife. He clobbers or comes to terms with puny Geras (Old Age) [*182*] and destroys the vineyard [*195*] or home [*363*] of *Syleus* who customarily exacted corvée from passers-by. (The Syleus scenes all fall between 490 and 460.) After 500 he is seen more often with Dionysos than hitherto. They may recline together [*376*] and satyrs often attend; or Herakles is alone with satyrs. In black figure he is shown capturing them, and where they appear robbing him of his arms while he sleeps we may suspect a satyr play theme.

The Herakles of red figure is less interesting than he had been in the sixth century, but his rival in the painter's repertory, Theseus, will never match his popularity with story-tellers in poetry or paint.

Theseus

The cycle of scenes depicting Theseus' adventures on the road from Troizen to claim his heritage in Athens only appear commonly on vases after about 510 and may be inspired by a new poem. They are a pallid but deliberate imitation of Herakles' Labours, and since the Herakles story seems to have been used by Peisistratos and his family, it is natural to find the new régime favouring a rival. The two heroes' relationship in myth, poetry, symbolism and religion is complicated, not hostile. Given the opportunities that myth provided it may be significant that no confrontations are admitted in these years, although their careers may be compared (as on the Athenian Treasury at Delphi) and only later, in play and art, is their association again presented. The Theseus stories are treated more as a cycle by artists than Herakles had been (although the Kleophrades Painter puts four Labours in one frieze), with single vases some-times illustrating several episodes. From *Periphetes* (or Korynetes – 'club-bearer') he acquired a club. *Sinis* challenged wayfarers to hold down a pine tree, bent to the ground, which soon sprang up to catapult and rend their bodies. Theseus deals with him in like way [*115, 206, 287*]. *Skiron* made folk wash his feet, then kicked them over the cliff to a tortoise/turtle waiting to eat them below. Theseus topples him [*90, 223*] and some scenes include all the paraphernalia – cliff, foot basin, turtle. *Prokrustes* lopped or stretched his victims to fit his beds. Theseus cuts him down to size, and the wood axe and bed may be shown [*137, 223, 319*]. *Phaia*, the savage sow of Krommyon, is killed [*287*]. *Kerkyon* of Eleusis, is wrestled. And later in Attica Theseus fights the Marathonian *Bull* [*201*]. The hero is usually lightly dressed in short chiton or with chlamys only, wearing a petasos travelling hat. Except with the bull he does not usually enjoy Athena's support (an interesting omission), but in some other scenes she is often shown.

The *Minotaur* story remains very popular, with the beast collapsing or being dragged from the palace-labyrinth: [*118*], cf. [*70*]. On the way to Crete Theseus had been challenged to prove that Poseidon was his father, and after 500 we find versions of his descent to the ocean-bed, supported by Triton, visiting the court of Poseidon and Amphitrite with their sea nymphs, and receiving a crown from *Amphitrite* [*223*]. Here Athena may attend. On his return from Crete the abandonment of the sleeping *Ariadne* on Naxos [*269*] is occasionally shown, even with an indication of her imminent discovery by Dionysos (Eros and the vine). Otherwise they are shown sleeping together or he is led from her, awake. There may also be the return to Athens.

Theseus had once carried off *Helen* [*34.1*] and his seizing of the Amazon *Antiope* appears early, as in black figure. At the end of our period and later there are some scenes of him threatening a woman, once named (by Makron) as Aithra, his mother. The occasion is not a recorded one, or else the inscription is a mistake (Aithra for another; Theseus for one of the Dioskouroi?). There are many scenes of him chasing unidentified young women, if all the youths dressed as Theseus are he.

The promotion of Theseus as the Athenian hero seems to have met with limited success with vase painters, beyond the cycle of pseudo-Labours, and more especially the Minotaur story (favoured long before) and the Bull episode in Attica itself. He may have fared better on walls and in verse.

Other heroes

PELEUS, whose major role is in the preliminaries to the Trojan cycle (below), is seen wrestling with *Atalanta* [*62*], an event at the funeral games of Pelias. She is shown naked but for an exercise cap, pants and a bra, but not always all three, and there are several studies of her alone [*369*]. On Douris' lekythos [*294*] her swift-footedness is the theme, and perhaps the love interest (the Erotes) lies in the foot race she set her suitors. She had also been at the Caly-donian boar hunt, but this is not a story to interest Archaic red figure artists as it had the black figure. We also lose sight for a while of Bellerophon.

PERSEUS killing Medusa or being pursued by her Gorgon sisters was most popular in black figure. In Archaic red figure we see a very few scenes of the pursuit (cf. [*153*, *349*]) but the hero's earlier life is now attended to. The Triptolemos Painter shows his mother *Danaë*, visited by Zeus' golden rain [*306*] and he and others have the chest being prepared for her voyage with baby Perseus by a carpenter (with bow drill) watched by King Akrisios [*192*]. There are one or two other versions of the scene with the chest, and later its recovery by fishermen.

JASON disgorged by a serpent before Athena on the Douris cup is an uncanonical episode from the Argonaut story [*288*]. For Medea's rejuvenation spells, vase painters show a ram being boiled [*200*], which in the texts is a

229

demonstration of power only. The spell is cast for *Pelias* before his daughters, and for Jason's father Aeson (given his son's name by mistake in [*200*]), but is rare.

OIDIPUS, confronting the sphinx on rock or column, is seen more often on later red figure [*301.2*]. ORPHEUS, clutching his lyre as he is torn by Thracian women, becomes quite a common figure after 500 [*277, 354*]. The weapons are usually domestic – spits, rocks, but a sword may be used, and a sickle to cut off his head. The youths sometimes present were his audience.

There are some minor pursuit scenes to set beside the Olympian. BOREAS AND OREITHYIA appear first at the end of our period [*341, 352*] (on the suggested symbolism see the start of this chapter). His hair is shaggy, sometimes later frosted and spiky. He is usually winged, as winds should be; and so is his son, young *Zephyros* pursuing the youth Hyakinthos or flying with him in his arms (but these identifications are less certain). Eos (Dawn), normally also winged, pursues either Kephalos [*203*], who is generally shown as a hunter (rarely as a schoolboy), with brimmed hat, chlamys and two spears, sometimes with his dog or dogs; or Tithonos [*379*], a handsome city boy for whom she negotiated immortality but not eternal youth. The favourite period for these pursuit scenes is from the end of the Archaic on.

A few scenes of about 500 and just afterwards show the arming of the SEVEN AGAINST THEBES. There is usually a chariot (for Amphiaraos) and common features are the attention paid to hair, holding a corselet, and signs of dejection. Parthenopaios is named on [*331*] to identify the group. The murder of AIGISTHOS by Orestes, with Klytaimnestra (rushing forward with an axe [*250*]) and Elektra, has the victim seated, sometimes with a lyre [*143, 274.2*]. Only the Dokimasia Painter, as a pendent to this, also shows the murder of Agamemnon [*274.1*], and in a near-Aeschylean manner already discussed.

The Trojan Cycle

Comparative study of the popular scenes from the Trojan cycle in black figure and red figure is revealing. After 530 black figure can still devote as many scenes to it as does red figure down to the mid fifth century, but the black figure total is due largely to the continuing popularity of a very few old favourites – Peleus and Thetis, Judgement of Paris, Troilos, Ajax carrying Achilles, Menelaos with Helen, Aeneas and Anchises, Polyphemos – while a number of other scenes are following the lead of red figure. On the other hand red figure more than doubles the number of subjects chosen. In so far as any preferences are shown they are for Achilles, especially in the first quarter of the fifth century when there is something of a boom in basic Trojan scenes, especially from the Iliad and Ilioupersis, and the record of the former is disproportionately due to the Kleophrades Painter's apparent interest in the

230

poem, plus the number of more domestic episodes shown by the Brygos Painter and his Circle. It really seems that in this field choice of subject is being far more often determined by knowledge of a text. This is a prelude to literary interests of later generations of painters, more open to influence from the stage than epic.

What follows is a summary of the scenes shown in Archaic red figure, following the order of the epic cycle, as in *ABFH* pp. 228–31. I have asterisked (★) those subjects whose iconography is in essence derived from the earlier black figure tradition.

KYPRIA. *Peleus wrestles Thetis*★ [*214.1*], versatile as ever, but the *Wedding* is now shown as a foot procession with the bride sometimes led in the ritual manner, hand upon wrist. The *child Achilles*★ is brought to Chiron for education [*56*]. The *Judgement of Paris*★ [*310*] has the hero now as a youth, no longer reluctant, with the rustic setting on Mount Ida more clearly indicated and the goddesses differentiated, Aphrodite often with attendant Eros or Erotes. *Paris leads Helen* away [*308.1*], but willingly, it seems, as a bride (hand on wrist) rather than victim, and his *return to Troy* is shown. On their way to Troy the Greeks mistakenly attacked the kingdom of *Telephos*. The king is wounded by Achilles and we see him seeking refuge at Agamemnon's court in Argos [*378*], only later seizing Orestes hostage. On the Trojan plain Achilles' pursuit of *Troilos*★ with his sister Polyxena [*190*] remains in the repertory, and there is more detail of Achilles dragging the boy from his horse by his hair and preparing to decapitate him beside Apollo's altar [*232*], but the waiting in ambush, so popular in black figure, is now rare.

ILIAD. There is far more attention in the early fifth century to episodes immediately connected with the poem's theme, the wrath of Achilles. We see the girl *Briseis* serving Phoinix (Achilles' mentor [*245.1*]), led away from Achilles by the heralds [*270*], delivered to Agamemnon. The *Mission to Achilles* [*166, 304.1*] shows the hero dejected, seated, head on hand and cloak over his head, before the appeasing heroes. These include Odysseus, seated clasping his knee or standing, Ajax, old Phoinix and (on vases but not in Homer) Diomedes. Achilles is silent, as in Aeschylus but not Homer, but it is far from clear that Aeschylus inspired the painters rather than epic. Achilles tends a wound of his companion Patroklos [*50.1*], and dispatches him to the field of battle where we see the fight over his body. The figure of *Achilles mourning* appears in scenes with Briseis led away, in the Mission and on later vases when his new armour is delivered and he is mourning Patroklos – almost generic studies of the tragic hero. Achilles' arming or rearming by Thetis [*332*] is no longer an important theme but there are several scenes in the 480's of *Thetis with Hephaistos* [*262.1*] receiving the new armour. Of the duels at Troy we see Ajax *v.* Hector★ [*304.2*], Ajax *v.* Aeneas (over Patroklos), Menelaos *v.* Paris, Diomedes *v.* Aeneas (with Athena encouraging and Aphrodite rescuing [*186*]) and Achilles *v.* Hector★ followed by the pursuit

231

round the walls. The Kleophrades Painter shows the exchange of gifts between *Ajax and Hector* and possibly the exchange of armour between Diomedes and Glaukos. The dragging of Hector is not a subject for red figure but the ransom is, with *Priam* and attendants bringing gifts of metal vessels and boxes for the rich robes mentioned by Homer for a nonchalant Achilles, Hector stretched out below his couch, a group best stated by the Brygos Painter [*248*]. Other episodes from the Iliad are the ambush of *Dolon* by Odysseus and Diomedes, with Dolon in his outlandish night-patrol gear [*276*]; and winged *Sleep and Death* carrying away the body of Sarpedon [*22*].

AITHIOPIS AND LITTLE ILIAD. The fight between *Achilles and Penthesilea*★ is remembered; and that between *Achilles and Memnon*★ remains important [*48.1*], where they may be seconded by their divine mothers or, for Achilles, Athena. Antilochos, Nestor's son, had been slain by Memnon, and is shown with his father and with Achilles. The *Psychostasia*★ of the lives of Achilles and Memnon [*134*] remains more popular than the Iliad's weighing for Achilles and Hector. *Eos*★ carries dead Memnon from the field [*292*].

Ajax carrying Achilles★, dead, is a far less popular theme now, but the sequel is not. *Ajax and Odysseus quarrel* [*247*] over Achilles' armour and are parted by their companions. The *voting* [*285.1*] is shown, before Athena, with the Greeks piling their pebble votes in Odysseus' favour and the heroes registering appropriate dismay and delight. The Brygos Painter shows *dead Ajax*, his body being covered by Tekmessa [*246*], laid on the fleeces of the rams he had slaughtered believing them, in his madness, to be Greeks. Odysseus' and Diomedes' removal of the *Palladion* from Troy is another late episode in the war [*185*]. Makron shows them quarrelling over it. The scene of *Achilles and Ajax*★ playing a board game [*2*] is not forgotten but hardly survives the Archaic period.

ILIOUPERSIS. Most of the standard scenes of the Sack of Troy were established in black figure and improved rather than altered in red figure: the *death of Priam*★, struck down by Neoptolemos on an altar, often with his grandson's body in evidence [*135.2, 245.2*]; the *rape of Kassandra*★ by the Lesser Ajax at the statue of Athena [*135.1*]; *Aeneas rescuing Anchises*★ with the child Askanios [*135.1*]; *Menelaos recovering Helen*★, threatening her with a sword [*308.2*], leading her away, and the first of the scenes with him dropping his sword at sight of her beauty [*158*]. A new figure is the Trojan woman, once named Andromache, who fights back with a pestle [*135.3*]; and a new story for art, the rescue of *Aithra* [*135.3, 172*], Theseus' mother who had gone to Troy as Helen's slave, by her grandsons. She is shown sometimes with cropped hair, as in Polygnotos' painting at Delphi, or as the 'vieille accroupie' of the Kleophrades Painter. The grouping of several episodes on one vase to provide a panorama of the Sack is a novelty, most subtly managed by the Kleophrades Painter [*135*]. The same artist may also show the rescue of *Antenor* who came to be regarded as a Trojan traitor for his conciliatory attitude towards the Greeks. Makron has *Polyxena* led to sacrifice.

ODYSSEY. The poem is almost ignored in Archaic red figure except for rare scenes in the old manner of *Circe*★, the escape from *Polyphemos*★, the *Sirens*★ [*184*]. Scenes with Penelope and the suitors come later.

Other figures

Several minor personifications, some novel, appear in Archaic red figure. *Dike fights Adikia* (Justice and Injustice) in red figure on an early bilingual, a theme which had appeared yet earlier on the chest of Kypselos at Olympia. *Selene* (the Moon) appears with her chariot, crowned by a disc like Isis, or perhaps as the head in a disc on the Sosias cup [*50.2*] and an Elpinikos Painter interior. There are also occasional *Tritons*, isolated [*217*] or helping Theseus under water [*223*], and Nereids with fish [*56, 61, 345*], not occupied by any specific story. The fights of *pygmies and cranes* had been favoured in earlier black figure, with the pygmies as tiny men. The Brygos Painter has them as realistic plump dwarfs [*258*]. In the underworld *Sisyphos* trundles his stone up hill and *Ixion* is pinned to his wheel on a few vases: subjects later ignored on Athenian vases.

The *Amazons* are extremely popular with as full a range of arming [*43*] and parade studies as are accorded male warriors. Their fights against Greeks (other than Herakles) only become really prolific in red figure after the Persian Wars. They are dressed as ordinary hoplites [*43*] or in Eastern garb as archers [*29*], or in decorative tunics [*9*], their femininity rarely being admitted. Several carry battle axes or are light-armed with crescent pelta shields.

Centaurs and the fight with centaurs will remain important subjects throughout the Classical period. On Archaic red figure the fight with the Lapiths, occasioned by the centaurs' unruly behaviour at the wedding of their king, is a set battle rather than the disturbance at the wedding [*170, 196, 268*]. So the Lapiths are armed and the invunerable *Kaineus* is shown beaten into the ground [*326*]. Theseus' help against the centaurs may have helped ensure the popularity of the subject in the early fifth century, but he is seldom explicitly identified.

Satyrs are the most engaging inventions of Greek art, never more entertaining than in the Archaic period and on red figure. They provide music and dance for Dionysos, alone or with their maenad companions. They play balancing tricks with their cups (at which they have special advantages [*299*]), or more usefully help at the vintage. For their role in myth we see them escorting Hephaistos to Olympus and assaulting goddesses. Silenos, the only individualised satyr, is led captive to King Midas. It would be easier to believe that armed satyrs [*31, 66, 140*] were preparing for the war against the Giants if there were more scenes of them fighting beside Dionysos. More enigmatic are isolated scenes of them destroying a tomb [*169*] or chopping up a herm.

233

The end of the sixth century sees the beginning of the satyr play in Athens, with actors dressed as satyrs, shaggy trunks holding on erect phallos and tail, fore and aft [314]. But our artists often ignore the costume and almost always the masks, in depicting what must be satyr play themes, the earliest of which (from about 510) seems to be their robbing of Herakles. Many of the new satyr scenes on vases, giving them family life [177, 301.1], as athletes [163] or involved in parody of myth, may derive, directly or indirectly, from their new stage role. The best of this comes later in the century but our [163, 174, 299, 325, 367] may be inspired by satyr plays.

The maenads with whom they dance wear animal skins over their ordinary clothes (as may any Dionysiac attendant), holding animals [40.2, 207] or snakes (and a snake hair band on [218]), or wielding the thyrsos wand, with its knob of ivy leaves [132.2], which may also be held by Dionysos or, less often, his satyrs. The maenads only undress to sleep. Some perform a winged dance by holding the cuffs of their loosened chiton sleeves in their hands [136, 271, 380]. They are often molested by the satyrs, but virtually never suffer the expected fate. A satyr's sexual release is generally self-administered. For him the pursuit is the thing, the excitement of the dance, the touch of thigh or arm, the impossibly heady pleasure of discovering or uncovering a maenad asleep [113, 257], but not the consummation. On the vases only mortals make it with their women. The satyrs act out mortal fantasies, mortal dreams which always seem to fade before fulfilment. They illustrate the timeless frustrations of the male, afflicted – or blessed – with permanent and unquenchable tumescence (they even infibulate on occasions), enjoying all the apparent pleasures and freedom of the good life. They are a more than adequate answer to those who believe that the Greeks were obsessed by homosexuality.

ABBREVIATIONS

AA	*Archäologischer Anzeiger*
AAA	*Athens Annals of Archaeology*
ABFH	J. Boardman, *Athenian Black Figure Vases, a Handbook* (1974)
ABL	E. Haspels, *Attic Black-figured Lekythoi* (1936)
ABV	J. D. Beazley, *Attic Black-figure Vase-painters* (1956)
ADelt	*Archaiologikon Deltion*
AE	*Archaiologike Ephemeris*
AJA	*American Journal of Archaeology*
AK	*Antike Kunst*
AM	*Athenische Mitteilungen*
Ann	*Annuario della Scuola Archeologica di Atene*
Arch. Class.	*Archeologia Classica*
ARV	J. D. Beazley, *Attic Red-figure Vase-painters* (1963)
BABesch	*Bulletin Antieke Beschaving*
BCH	*Bulletin de Correspondance Hellénique*
Boston	L. D. Caskey and J. D. Beazley, *Attic Vase Paintings in the Museum of Fine Arts, Boston*
BSA	*Annual of the British School at Athens*
CVA	*Corpus Vasorum Antiquorum*
Hesp	*Hesperia*
HGVP	P. Arias, M. Hirmer, B. B. Shefton, *History of Greek Vase Painting* (1962)
JdI	*Jahrbuch des deutschen archäologischen Instituts*
JHS	*Journal of Hellenic Studies*
MJBK	*Münchener Jahrbuch der bildenden Kunst*
MonPiot	*Monuments et Mémoires, Fondation Piot*
MWPr	*Marburger Winckelmanns-programm*
ÖJh	*Jahreshefte des österreichischen archäologischen Instituts in Wien*
Para	J. D. Beazley, *Paralipomena* (1971)
RA	*Revue Archéologique*
RM	*Römische Mitteilungen*
VAmer	J. D. Beazley, *Attic Red-figured Vases in American Museums* (1918)
VPol	J. D. Beazley, *Greek Vases in Poland* (1928)

NOTES AND BIBLIOGRAPHIES

GENERAL BOOKS

J. D. Beazley, *ARV* for full lists of painters and indexes to provenience, myth, museums, kalos names; supplemented in *Para*. M. Robertson's review article of *ARV* in *JHS* lxxxv, 90ff. is important.

Beazley, *VAmer* introduces with brief discussion many painters and groups.

A. Furtwängler and K. Reichhold, *Griechische Vasenmalerei* i–iii (1900–32), important essays and illustration of select vases.

J. C. Hoppin, *A Handbook of Greek Red Figured Vases* (1919) for pictures (old) of signed and some attributed vases.

E. Pfuhl, *Malerei und Zeichnung der Griechen* (1923), a comprehensive survey, outdated.

A. Rumpf, *Malerei und Zeichnung* (1953), packed, informative and sensible discussion with very small pictures.

G. M. A. Richter, *Attic Red-Figured Vases, a Survey* (1958), good and fairly detailed general discussion of development and painters with few small pictures.

M. Robertson, *Greek Painting* (1959), excellent text with all colour pictures.

B. B. Shefton in *HGVP*, good descriptions of good large photographs (Hirmer) and summaries of some painters' careers.

R. M. Cook, *Greek Painted Pottery* (1972), Chapter 5.

R. Lullies and M. Hirmer, *Griechische Vasen der reifarchaischen Zeit* (1953), good photographs and discussion of a very rich collection (Munich).

Enciclopedia dell'Arte antica (1958–66), brief accounts of painters and subjects.

H. Metzger gives valuable biennial summaries of recent work on Greek vases in *Revue des Études grecques*, since 1960.

Kerameus, a new series of monographs devoted to studies of painters with comprehensive illustration (von Zabern).

For the best full account of the vases in the general context of Greek art see M. Robertson, *History of Greek Art* (Cambridge, 1975).

CVA publishes pictures of all decorated Greek vases by museum. Most series remain incomplete

and the older volumes have poor or small pictures. Those of Oxford (Beazley), London, Munich and the post-war volumes are the best.

Other publications of important collections of red figure with reliable texts are:

J. D. Beazley (and L. D. Caskey for i), *Boston* i–iii (1931–63).

G. M. A. Richter and L. F. Hall, *Red-figured Athenian Vases in the Metropolitan Museum of Art* (1936).

E. Langlotz, *Griechische Vasen in Würzburg* (1932).

B. Graef and E. Langlotz, *Die antiken Vasen von der Akropolis zu Athen* ii.

I. INTRODUCTION

History – R. M. Cook in *Greek Painted Pottery* ch. 15.

M. Robertson, *Between Archaeology and Art History* (1963).

J. D. Beazley, *Potter and Painter in Ancient Athens* (1944).

I owe observations on Euphronios and Hygieia to Jody Maxmin; on Persepolis to Michael Roaf.

Wall paintings: Paestum – M. Napoli, *La Tomba del Tuffatore* (1970); Elmali – M. Mellink, *AJA* lxxiv–lxxvii.

The reader is invited to turn to *ARV* and *Para* for the fullest bibliographies of painters and vases. I give references to useful discussions or illustrations, to recent works or to some particular points raised in the text.

II. THE FIRST GENERATION

THE RED FIGURE TECHNIQUE

Preliminary sketch – P. E. Corbett, *JHS* lxxxv, 16ff.; R. D. de Puma, *AJA* lxxii, 152–4 (Makron).

Relief line – see Beazley's descriptions in *Boston* and *CVA* Oxford.

Technique – J. V. Noble, *The Techniques of Painted Attic Pottery* (1965).

Siphnian Treasury – R. Lullies and M. Hirmer, *Greek Sculpture* (1960) pls. 48–55; D. von Bothmer, *Metr. Mus. Bull.* xxiv, 208–10; E. Langlotz, *Zeitbestimmung* 17ff.

And black figure – *ABFH* 103f.; M. Robertson, *AK* Beiheft ix, 83f.

INVENTION AND EXPERIMENT

ANDOKIDES PAINTER

H. Bloesch, *JHS* lxxi, 30f. (the potter); A. Marwitz, *ÖJh* xlvi, 73ff.; K. Schauenburg, *JdI* lxxvi, 48ff. (61ff. on identity), lxxx, 92ff.; G. Szilagyi, *Bull. du Mus. Hongroise* xxviii, 13ff.; *Boston* iii, 1–7; D. von Bothmer, *Metr. Mus. Bull.* xxiv, 201ff.; A. Büsing-Kolbe, *MWPr* 1971/2, 60ff. (fragment, near); *HGVP* 316f.; *ABFH* 105.

PSIAX

VAmer 6; G. M. A. Richter, *AJA* xxxviii, 547ff., xlv, 587ff.; H. R. W. Smith, *New Aspects of the Menon Painter* (1929); *ABL* 77 (connection with later artists); *ABFH* 106; S. P. Uggeri, *Num. e Ant. Class.* 1972, 33ff. D. C. Kurtz, forthcoming.

PASEAS

C. Roebuck, *AJA* xliii, 467ff.; Boardman, *JHS* lxxv, 154f. and *ABFH* 106; A. Greifenhagen, *Jb. Berliner Museen* iii, 117ff. and forthcoming on the w.g. plaque; D. C. Kurtz, forthcoming. Akr. ii, no. 1040, pl. 81 (erotic plaque [*18*]); no. 199, pl. 9 (r.f. with coral-red background); i, no. 2499, pl. 102 (r.f. plaque with white background; the other side b.f.; *ABV* 506).

Goluchow Painter – *VPol* 11ff.; R. D. Blatter, *AA* 1972, 237ff.

THE PIONEERS

GENERAL

VAmer 27ff.; Beazley, *Potter and Painter in Ancient Athens* 19ff.; A. Greifenhagen, *Jb. Berliner Museen* ix, 10ff. (Smikros kalos); E. Vermeule, *AK* xiii, 35 (Smikros and Euphronios); *Boston* ii, 4f. (Phayllos); M. Ohly-Dumm, forthcoming.

EUPHRONIOS

F. P. Johnson, *Art Bulletin* xix, 557ff.; F. Villard, *MonPiot* xlv, 1ff., xlvii, 35ff. (askoliasmos); E. Vermeule, *AK* viii, 34ff. and D. Ohly, *MJBK* xxii, 229ff. (Munich crater with Smikros); D. von Bothmer, *Metr. Mus. Bull.* xxxi, 1ff.; J. Maxmin, *AAA* vi, 299ff. (anatomy); *HGVP* 323–6; D. von Bothmer, forthcoming.

SMIKROS

C. Gaspar, *MonPiot* ix, 15ff.; A. Greifenhagen, *Jb. Berliner Museen* ix, 10ff.; *HGVP* 322f.

EUTHYMIDES

J. C. Hoppin, *Euthymides and his Fellows* (1917) reviewed by Beazley, *JHS* xxxvii, 233ff.; *HGVP* 326–8.

Phintias – Hoppin, op. cit., 93ff.; *HGVP* 317–19.
Hypsis – Hoppin, op. cit., 135ff.
Sosias Painter – *CVA* Berlin ii, pls. 49, 50.

Gotha cup – *CVA* Gotha i, 54, pls. 42, 43.
Pioneer black figure, etc.: Euthymidean w.g. plaques – [*52*, *53*], *ARV* 1598, Boardman, *JHS* lxxvi, 20–2; b.f. plaques – Akr. i, no. 2514 (K. Peters, *Panath. Preisamphoren* 56, as Euphronios; ? better Euthymides); Panathenaics – Akr. i, no. 931 (Peters, loc. cit.; *ARV* 18); Pioneer r.f. plaques – Akr. ii, no. 1042 (Boardman, *JHS* lxxvi, 22f.).

CUP PAINTERS

GENERAL

P. Hartwig, *Die griechischen Meisterschalen* (1893), important early study of hands and groups; H. Bloesch, *Formen attischer Schalen* (1940), pioneer study of shapes; *ARV* 39f., classification of eye cups; E. Haspels, *BCH* liv (1930) 23ff., parade cups; *Athenian Agora* xii, 91f., Type C; coral-red, gilding, etc. – ibid., 19–21 and A. Winter, *AM* lxxxiii, 315f.; tondo composition – C. Rolley, *RA* 1972, 151ff.

OLTOS

F. P. Johnson, *Art Bulletin* xix, 537ff.; A. Bruhn, *Oltos* (1943); *HGVP* 320f.

EPIKTETOS

VAmer 14–18; W. Kraiker, *JdI* xliv, 141ff.; M. Robertson, *JHS* lxxxv, 99f. (late work); *HGVP* 319f.; Boardman, forthcoming.

Pheidippos – W. Kraiker, *AM* lv, 107ff.

SKYTHES

VAmer 21f.; E. Pottier, *MonPiot* ix, 135ff., x, 49ff.; G. E. Rizzo, *MonPiot* xx, 101ff.; *ABV* 352 (b.f. plaques).

EUERGIDES PAINTER

Beazley, *JHS* xxxiii, 347ff.; *ARV* 1631 (?=Delos P.); D. von Bothmer, *RA* 1972, 83ff. (hemicylindrical stands).

EPELEIOS PAINTER

For comparisons with Epiktetos take *ARV* 150, 37 (probably his) and *ARV* 76, 84. Better than usual is *CVA* Bryn Mawr i, pls. 3, 4; *ARV* 147, 18.
Paidikos Alabastra and Pasiades – *ABL* 101–4.
Hermaios Painter – W. Kraiker, *AA* 1923/24, 165ff.
Apollodoros – M. Ohly-Dumm, *MJBK* xxii, 7ff. (Elpinikos P.).
Ambrosios Painter – *VAmer* 19f.

III. THE LATE ARCHAIC PAINTERS

THE KLEOPHRADES PAINTER AND THE BERLIN PAINTER

KLEOPHRADES PAINTER

Beazley, *JHS* xxx, 38ff., *VAmer* 40–4, *The Kleophrades Painter* (1974) and *AK* i, 6–8; G. M. A. Richter, *AJA* xl, 100ff. ('Epiktetos II'); L. Schnitzler, *Opusc. Ath.* xi, 47ff. (a Corinthian); R. Lullies, *Die Spitzamphora des Kleophrades Malers* (1957) and forthcoming, A. II. Ashmead, *Hesp* xxxv, 20ff. (Athens frr.); U. Knigge, *AM* lxxxv, 1ff. (Athens frr.); *HGVP* 328–31; A. Greifenhagen, *Neue Fragmente des Kleophrades Malers* (1972); Boardman, *Getty Museum Annual* i, *AA* 1981, 329ff.

BERLIN PAINTER

Beazley, *JHS* xxxi, 276ff. and xlii, 70ff., *The Berlin Painter* (Melbourne, 1964), *MonPiot* xxxv, 64ff., *AK* iv, 49ff., *The Berlin Painter* (1974); M. Robertson, *JHS* lxx, 23ff. (origins), *AJA* lxii, 55ff. (Gorgos) and forthcoming; R. H. Blatter, *AK* v, 18ff. (potter); R. Lullies, *AK* xiv, 44ff. (dinos); C. Isler-Kerenyi, *AK* xiv, 25ff. (Nolans, Nike); H. Giroux, *RA* 1972, 243ff. (volute crater *ARV* nos. 129 + 130); Byvanck-van Ufford, *RA* 1972, 20ff. (archaising); *HGVP* 343–5; M. Schmidt, forthcoming on [*149*].

OTHER POT PAINTERS

Nikoxenos Painter – Beazley, *BSA* xix, 229ff. and *VAmer* 25f.; M. Robertson, *AJA* lxvi, 311f.
Eucharides Painter – Beazley, *BSA* xviii, 217ff. and xix, 245, *VAmer* 45–7; M. Robertson, *Getty Museum Annual* i.
Myson – *VAmer* 48–52; *HGVP* 332.
Harrow Painter – Beazley, *JHS* xxxvi, 128f. and *VAmer* 57; *ARV* 1635f., 1705 (and Berlin P.).
Flying Angel Painter – *Boston* iii, 16f.
Tyszkiewicz Painter – Beazley, *AJA* xx, 144ff., *VAmer* 55.
Troilos Painter – Beazley, *JHS* xxxii, 172f., *ARV* 1643.
Syleus Sequence – *VAmer* 52, 66f.; *Boston* ii, 11–13; M. Robertson, *AK* xiii, 13ff. (for unity) and forthcoming.
Syriskos Group – *VAmer* 63–5; B. Philippaki, *The Attic Stamnos* 63ff.; *Para* 352f. (P. S. Painter).
Negro Alabastra – H. Winnefeld, *AM* xiv, 41ff.; A. D. Fraser, *AJA* xxxix, 41ff.; *ABL* 103f.
Lekythoi – *ABL* 69–76 (r.f.), 110–13 (semi-outline); *ARV* 1644.
Dutuit Painter – Beazley, *JHS* xxxiii, 106ff.
Tithonos Painter – *VAmer* 69f.

CUP PAINTERS

See general bibliography in last chapter. Acrocup – *Boston* ii, 67.

WHITE GROUND

H. Philippart, *Ant. Class.* v, 5ff., lists and pictures; A. Waiblinger, *RA* 1972, 233ff. (Onesiman); J. R. Mertens, *Harvard Stud. Class. Phil.* lxxvi, 271ff. (Euphronios?).

ONESIMOS

VAmer 82–9; *VPol* 21–3; *ARV* 312f.; *Boston* ii, 23–36; *HGVP* 333–5; H. van Lucken in *Gr. Vasen* (Rostock) 485ff. (divisory); J. Maffre, *RA* 1972, 221ff.

Antiphon Painter – *VAmer* 111f.; R. Blatter, *AA* 1968, 640ff.

BRYGOS PAINTER

VAmer 89–93; G. M. A. Richter in *Charites* (Fest. Langlotz) 141; *HGVP* 336–9; A. M. Tamassia, *Boll. d'Arte* lii, 1–9; A. Cambitoglou, *The Brygos Painter* (1968); M. Wegner, *Der Brygosmaler* (1973).

FOUNDRY PAINTER

H. A. Thompson in *Essays Karl Lehmann* 323ff. (name cup); Beazley, *Un Realista greco* (1966).

Briseis Painter – *VAmer* 109f.
Dokimasia Painter – E. Vermeule, *AJA* lxx, 1ff. (Boston crater).
Painter of Paris Gigantomachy – *VAmer* 94f.

DOURIS

VAmer 97–100; *ARV* 425–7; Beazley, *JHS* xxxix, 84f.; *HGVP* 339–43; B. Philippaki in *Kernos* (Fest. Bakalakis) 197ff. (signed aryballos); M. Wegner, *Duris* (1968).

TRIPTOLEMOS PAINTER

Beazley, *Painter and Potter* 41 (Douris signature) and in *Charites* 138f.; E. R. Knauer, *Ein Skyphos des Triptolemos-malers* (1973).

Makron – *V Amer* 101f.; Beazley, *AJA* xxv, 330ff., *BSA* xxix, 193 and *Boston* iii, 30ff.; *HGVP* 332f.

IV. MANNERISTS AND OTHERS

MANNERISTS

Beazley, *Potter and Painter* 13; *VPol* 40; *The Pan Painter* (1974) 8f.
Leningrad Painter – J. R. Green, *JHS* lxxxi, 73–5 (vase studio [*323*]).

PAN PAINTER

Beazley, *JHS* xxxii, 354ff., *VAmer* 113–18, *Boston* ii, 45–55, *The Pan Painter* (1974); *HGVP* 346f.; L. Jehasse, *MonPiot* lviii, 25ff.; A. B. Follmann, *Der Pan Maler* (1968) and in *Gr. Vasen* (Rostock) 445ff.; Byvanck-van Ufford, *BABesch* xliv, 124ff. (downdates early career).

POT PAINTERS

Painter of Munich 2413 – *VAmer* 123f. (as Hermonax).

HERMONAX

VAmer 123f.; F. P. Johnson, *AJA* xlix, 491ff. (late), lii, 233ff.; N. Weill, *BCH* lxxxvi, 64ff.; M. Pallottino, *Mem. della R. Acc. d'It.* vii, 1; B. B. Shefton, forthcoming.

Providence Painter – *VAmer* 76f.; *VPol* 16f.; *Boston* ii, 41–5.

CUP PAINTERS

Euaion Painter – *VAmer* 157f.; *VPol* 46f.

Telephos Painter – *VAmer* 107–9; *VPol* 38f.; C. S. Nobile, *Il pittore di Telefo* (1969).
Boot Painter – *VPol* 37; *ARV* 821.

V. SHAPES AND DATES

SHAPES

G. M. A. Richter and M. J. Milne, *Shapes and Names of Athenian Vases* (1935), a usefully illustrated guide. J. V. Noble, *The Techniques of Painted Attic Pottery* (1965) 11ff. L. Talcott and B. A. Sparkes, *Athenian Agora* xii, for black shapes but most relevant. H. Gericke, *Gefässdarstellungen auf gr. Vasen* (1970) for vases on vases.
I cite also *CVA*'s where a good range of illustrations may be found.
See *ABFH* 237f., adding:
Alabastron – U. Knigge, *AM* lxxix, 109ff.; K. Schauenburg, *JdI* lxxxvii, 259ff.
Amphora, belly – R. Lullies, *AK* vii, 85ff.; Type A, *Boston* iii, 1; Type C, *Boston* iii, 16; *CVA* Louvre v, Munich iv, London iii.
Amphora, neck – Beazley, *BSA* xviii, 217ff.; Nolans, *VAmer* 37f., *Boston* ii, 39f. (470's); *CVA* Vienna ii, Louvre vi, Munich iv, London iii, v (Nolans).
Aryballos – Beazley, *BSA* xxix, 187f., 193ff.; Haspels, ibid., 216ff. on carrying.
Askos – Beazley, *AJA* xxv, 326f.; G. Snijder, *Mnemosyne* 1934, 34ff.
Crater, bell – *Boston* ii, 50; *Athenian Agora* xii, 55; A. B. Follmann, *Der Pan Maler* 50f.
Crater, calyx – C. Boulter, *AK* vi, 71.
Crater, column – *CVA* Vienna ii, Bologna i.
Crater, volute – *Boston* ii, 80.
Cup – see bibliographies for other chs.; *CVA* Vienna i, Louvre x, Berlin ii, iii, Adria i, Florence iii, iv, Robinson Coll. ii, Bryn Mawr i.
Hydria – *Boston* ii, 9f. (b.f. shape); Follmann, op. cit., 49f. (kalpis); *CVA* Paris vi, Munich v, London v.
Kalathos – R. T. Williams, *AK* iv, 27ff.
Kantharos – *Boston* i, 14–18, iii, 10f., 52f.; D. Feytmans, *Ant. Class.* xiv, 314ff. (Type C); *CVA* London iv.
Lekythos – D. C. Kurtz, *Athenian White Lekythoi* (1975); W. W. Rudolph, *Die Bauchlekythos* (1971); *CVA* Palermo (Mormino) i.
Oinochoe – J. R. Green, *Bull. Inst. Class. London* xix, 1ff.; K. Peters, *JdI* lxxxvi, 114ff. (chous); *CVA* Munich ii, Berlin iii.
Pelike – *CVA* Vienna ii, Louvre vi, Athens (forthcoming).
Psykter – Follmann, op. cit., 27f.
Skyphos – F. P. Johnson in *Studies Robinson* ii, 96ff. and *AJA* lix, 119ff. (Type B); *CVA* Vienna i, Berlin iii, London iv.
Stamnos – *CVA* Munich v, London iii.
Stand, hemicylindrical – D. von Bothmer, *RA* 1972, 83ff.

DATES

E. Langlotz, *Zur Zeitbestimmung der strengrotfigurigen Vasenmalerei und der gleichzeitigen Plastik* (1920); Athens, Agora – *Athenian Agora* xii, 383ff. for deposits; Athens, Acropolis – W. B. Dinsmoor, *AJA* xxxviii, 408ff.; Follmann, op. cit., 20ff.; Eion herms – J. de la Genière, *Rev. Et. Anc.* lxii, 249ff.; ostraka – A. Greifenhagen, *Neue Fragmente.* 22f. and D. M. Lewis, *Zeitschr. Pap. Epigr.* xiv, 1–4.

VI. GENERAL DECORATION

CONVENTIONS

Gestures – G. Neumann, *Gesten und Gebärden* (1965); G. M. A. Richter, *Perspective in Greek and Roman Art* (1970).

INSCRIPTIONS

Beazley's articles on Some Inscriptions on Vases indicate the wealth of interest here, yet to be systematically explored: *AJA* xxxi, 345ff.; xxxiii, 361ff.; xxxix, 475ff.; xlv, 593ff.; liv, 310ff.; lviii, 187ff.; lxi, 5ff.; lxiv, 219ff. H. Immerwahr promises a comprehensive study.
Kalos names – D. M. Robinson and J. Fluck, *A Study of the Greek Love Names* (1937); J. K. Davies, *Athenian Propertied Families* (1971); lists in *ARV* 1559ff. and *Para* 505ff.

FLORALS AND ORNAMENT

P. Jacobsthal, *Ornamente griechischer Vasen* (1927); D. C. Kurtz, *Athenian White Lekythoi* (1975).

ANIMALS AND MONSTERS

Deer – F. Brein, *Der Hirsch in der gr. Frühzeit* (1969).
Dokimasia – H. Cahn, *RA* 1973, 3ff.
Dolphin riders – F. Brommer, *AA* 1942, 65ff.
Felines – W. L. Brown, *The Etruscan Lion* (1960) 170ff.
Foxes – K. Schauenburg, *AM* lxxxvi, 47f.
Horses and Hunting – J. K. Anderson, *Ancient Greek Horsemanship* (1961).
Martens – *Boston* iii, 29.
Mixed monsters – Boardman, *Archaic Greek Gems* (1968) 105, 154–7.
Owls – J. H. Jongkees, *Mnemosyne* 1952, 28ff.

VII. SCENES OF REALITY

See *ABFH* 239.

EVERYDAY LIFE

Dress – (add for b.f. P. C. Cecchetti in *Studi Misc.* xix); P. Wolters, *Faden und Knoten als Amulett*; A. Krug, *Binden in der gr. Kunst* (1968).
Washing – R. Ginouvès, *Balaneutiké* (1962).
See-saw – *Boston* iii, 48f.
Toy chariots – Beazley, *BSA* xxix, 187ff. on [*318*].

239

Scrolls on vases – H. Immerwahr in *Studies Ullman* i, 17ff. and *AK* xvi, 143.
Caricatures – V. Zinserling in *Gr. Vasen* (Rostock) 571ff.
Easterners – L. Schnitzler, *Zeitschr. d. deutsch. morgenländ. Ges.* xxxiii, 54ff.

FIGHTING

A. M. Snodgrass, *Arms and Armour of the Greeks* (1967); add for b.f., P. A. L. Greenhalgh, *Early Greek Warfare* (1973) on horsemen and chariots.
Helmets – *Boston* ii, 20 (decoration); B. Schröder, *JdI* xxvii, 317ff. (Thracian).
Dress – A. Bovon, *BCH* lxxxvii, 579ff. (Persian); H. Cahn, *RA* 1973, 13f. (Thracian); W. van Ingen, *HarvardStud. Class. Phil.* xlvi, 162 (apron); Boardman, *Class. Quarterly* 1973, 196f. (hair); K. Schauenburg, *Ant. und Abendland* xx, 88ff. (Thracian).
Machaira – G. Roux, *AK* vii, 30ff.
Testing arrows, bows – *Boston* ii, 28.
Dancers – J. Poursat, *BCH* xcii, 550ff.

ENTERTAINMENT

A. Pickard-Cambridge, *The Dramatic Festivals of Athens* (1968); M. Schmidt, *AK* x, 70ff. (choruses).
P. Jacobsthal, 'Symposiaka' in *Göttinger Vasen* (1912).
Kottabos – B. A. Sparkes, *Archaeology* xiii, 202ff.
Anakreon – *Boston* ii, 55–61; D. C. Kurtz/J. Boardman, *Vases in Getty Mus*, iii, 35ff.
Pyrrhic dancers – Poursat, loc. cit.
Music – M. Wegner, *Musikgeschichte in Bildern* (1964); U. Klein, *Gymnasium* lxxiv, 139ff. (horns).
Balancing – *Boston* ii, 26.
Love-making – G. Vorberg, *Glossarium Eroticum* (1965); H. Licht, *Sittengeschichte Griechenlands* (1925–8); E. Vermeule, *AK* xii, 9ff. (Boston) and *AJA* lxxi, 311ff.; Boardman in *European Community in Prehistory* (Studies Hawkes) 136f.
Phallos birds – R. Herter in Pauly-Wissowa s.v. 'Phallos' 1724f.; G. Devereux, *JHS* xciii, 42f.

SPORT

E. N. Gardiner, *Athletics of the Ancient World* (1930); H. A. Harris, *Sport in Greece and Rome* (1972).
Boston i, 13 (athletes with fillets); ii, 3f. (acontists).

COMMERCE AND INDUSTRY

P. Cloche, *Les classes, les métiers, le trafic* (1931).
Pottery – G. M. A. Richter, *The Craft of Athenian Pottery* (1923).
Sculpture – *Boston* iii, 74f.
Metal Vases – J. R. Green, *JHS* lxxxi, 73–5.
Rustic dress – *Boston* ii, 48f.; iii, 56.

RELIGION

L. Deubner, *Attische Feste* (1932).
Herms – R. Lullies, *Die Typen der gr. Herme* (1931); P. Devambez, *RA* 1968, 139ff.

Sacrifice and cooking – G. Rizza, *Ann.* xxxvii/xxxviii, 321ff.
Burial – D. C. Kurtz and J. Boardman, *Greek Burial Customs* (1971).
Votive plaques – Boardman, *BSA* xlix, 186ff.; Akr. ii, nos. 1038ff.

HISTORICAL FIGURES

T. Hölscher, *Gr. Historienbilder des 5. und 4. Jdts.* (1973); *AK* xvii, 78ff. (Greeks *v.* Persians).

VIII. SCENES OF MYTH

See *ABFH* 239–41 for many relevant references, few of which are repeated here.
F. Brommer, *Vasenlisten zur gr. Heldensage*³ (1973) for full lists and bibliography, without commentary; and indexes to *ARV* and *Para*. Encyclopaedia sources are: W. H. Roscher's *Lexicon* (a new *Lexicon Iconographicum Mythologiae Classicae* is being prepared); and more recently *Enciclopedia dell'Arte antica* (1958–66), *Lexikon der alten Welt* (1965) and the *Oxford Classical Dictionary* (1970).
Red figure iconography has been studied by scholars no less thoroughly than that of earlier periods, but more piecemeal. The following references supplement the major sources given above. Articles cited in *ABFH* are not generally repeated here, so most entries are either primarily r.f. interest, or more recent than *ABFH*.

THE GODS

E. Simon, *Die Götter der Griechen* (1969) and *Opfernde Götter* (1953), on libations; G. Beckel, *Götterbeistand* (1961).

ZEUS

A. B. Cook, *Zeus* i–iii (1914–40); D. Aebli, *Klassischer Zeus* (1971).
Ganymede – *Boston* ii, 51–3; H. Sichtermann, *AK* ii, 10ff.
Pursues Thetis – *Boston* ii, 68f.

APOLLO

Marpessa – Beazley in *Charites* (Fest. Langlotz) 136–9.
Hyakinthos – H. Sichtermann, *JdI* lxxi, 97ff.

HERMES

P. Zanker, *Wandel der Hermesgestalt in der attischen Vasenmalerei* (1965).

DIONYSOS

Pentheus – *Boston* ii, 1–3.
Rape of Hera and Iris – *ABL* 20; A. Cambitoglou, *The Brygos Painter* 20–3.

HEPHAISTOS

Forge – R. D. Gempeler, *AK* xii, 16ff.

POSEIDON

U. Heimberg, *Das Bild des Poseidon* (1968).

Amymone – F. Brommer, *AM* lxiii/lxiv, 171ff.; *Boston* ii, 89–92.

ATHENA
Erichthonios- Brommer in *Charites* (Fest. Langlotz) 157f.

NIKE
C. Isler-Kerenyi, *Nike* (1969) and *AK* xiv, 27ff.

DEMETER
H. Metzger, *Recherches sur l'Imagerie Athénienne* (1965) 7ff.; A. Peschlow-Bindokat, *JdI* lxxxvii, 60ff.

EROS
A. Greifenhagen, *Griechische Eroten* (1957).

ARTEMIS
Aktaion – *Boston* ii, 47f., 83–6; K. Schauenburg, *JdI* lxxxiv, 29ff.; P. Devambez, *MonPiot* lv, 77ff.

PAN
F. Brommer, *Marburger Jb. Kunstwiss.* xv, 15ff.

HERAKLES
F. Brommer, *Herakles* (1953), mainly on the Labours; R. Flacelière and P. Devambez, *Hérakles, Images et Récits* (1966).
v. Apollo, deer – F. Brommer, *AK* Beiheft vii, 51–3.
v. Busiris – Felletti Maj, *Riv. Ist. Arch.* vi, 207ff.
v. Geras – G. Hafner, *Röm. Germ. Zentralmus. Mainz* v, 139ff.; Beazley, *BABesch* xxiv/xxvi, 18ff.
and Hesperides – A. Greifenhagen, *Neue Fragmente des Kleophradesmalers* 35ff.
v. Kerberos – F. Brommer, *AK* Beiheft vii, 50f.
and satyrs, robbed – Beazley, *Apollo* (Salerno) iii/iv, 3ff.
v. snakes – O. Brendel, *JdI* xlvii, 191ff.
v. Syleus – F. Brommer, *JdI* lix/lx, 69ff.

THESEUS
C. Dugas and R. Flacelière, *Thesée, Images et Récits* (1958); C. Dugas, *Rev. Et. Gr.* lvi, 1ff.
Amphitrite – P. Jacobsthal, *Theseus auf dem Meeresgrunde* (1911).
v. Minotaur – F. Brommer, *AK* Beiheft vii, 53f.
v. Sinis – G. Hafner, *AA* 1966, 151ff.
chases woman – *Boston* ii, 81f.
lifts stone – C. Sourvinou-Inwood, *JHS* xci, 94ff.

OTHER HEROES
Atalanta – E. Simon, *Meleager und Atalante* (1970).
Perseus – K. Schauenburg, *Perseus* (1960).
Danaë – *Boston* ii, 11f.; S. Karouzou, *BCH* lxx, 436ff. and *AK* xiii, 36ff.; T. P. Howe, *AJA* lvii, 269ff.
Orpheus – *Boston* ii, 72–6; F. M. Schoeller, *Darstellungen des Orpheus in der Antike* (1969); M. Schmidt, *AK* Beiheft vii, 95ff.
Boreas and Oreithyia – E. Simon, *Antike und Abendland* xiii, 111ff.
Eos and Kephalos/Tithonos – *Boston* ii, 37f.

Seven against Thebes – Beazley, *AJA* liv, 313; G. M. A. Richter, *AJA* lxxiv, 331ff.
Aigisthos, Agamemnon – E. Vermeule, *AJA* lxx, 1ff.; M. Davies, *BCH* xciii, 214ff.; *Opusc. Rom.* ix, 117ff.

THE TROJAN CYCLE
K. F. Johansen, *The Iliad in Early Greek Art* (1967); M. R. Scherer, *The Legends of Troy* (1963).
Judgement of Paris – C. Clairmont, *Das Parisurteil in der antiken Kunst* (1951); T. C. W. Stinton, *Euripides and the Judgement of Paris* (1965); I. Raab, *Zu den Darstellungen des Parisurteils in der gr. Kunst* (1972).
Marriage of Peleus and Thetis – E. Haspels, *BCH* liv, 422ff.
Marriage of Menelaos and Helen – *Boston* ii, 43f.
Telephos – *Boston* iii, 54–7; C. Bauchhenss-Thürtiedl, *Der Mythos von Telephos* (1971).
Troilos – C. Mota, *RA* 1957, 25ff.; N. Kunisch, *AA* 1965, 394ff.
Mission to Achilles – M. Schmidt in *Opus Nobile* (Fest. Jantzen) 141ff.; B. Döhle, *Klio* xlix, 99ff.
Hephaistos and Thetis – *Boston* ii, 36.
Achilles *v.* Penthesilea – U. Hausmann, *AA* 1965, 150ff.
Diomedes *v.* Aeneas – *Boston* ii, 19f.; Boardman, *Getty Museum Annual* i.
Psychostasia – E. Simon, *Die Geburt der Aphrodite* (1959) 72ff., 110; C. C. van Essen, *BABesch* xxxix, 126–8.
Achilles *v.* Memnon – *Boston* ii, 14–19.
Quarrel over armour and voting – M. Davies, *AK* xvi, 67ff.
Ajax dead – M. Davies, *AK* xvi, 60ff.; B. B. Shefton, *RA* 1973, 203ff.
Rape of Kassandra – *Boston* iii, 61–5.
Menelaos and Helen – L. Ghali-Kahil, *Les enlèvements et le retour d'Hélène* (1955).
Odyssey – O. Touchefeu-Meynier, *Thèmes odysséens dans l'art antique* (1968).

OTHER FIGURES
Personifications – F. W. Hamdorf, *Gr. Kultpersonifikationen* (1964).
Dike, Adikia – J. Frel in *Geras* (Studies Thompson) 95ff.
Selene – F. Brommer, *AA* 1963, 680ff.
Amazons – D. von Bothmer, *Amazons in Greek Art* (1957).
Centaurs – P. V. C. Baur, *Centaurs in Ancient Art* (1912).
Satyrs – F. Brommer, *Satyroi* (1937) and *Satyrspiele* (1959); *Boston* ii, 71f. (in biga), ii, 95–9 (approaching maenad); E. Pottier, *MonPiot* xxix, 149ff. and C. Bérard, *AK* ix, 93ff. (breaking herm, tomb); K. Schauenburg, *JdI* lxxxviii, 1ff. (at feast).
Maenads – M. W. Edwards, *JHS* lxxx, 78ff.
Silenos and Midas – F. Brommer, *AK* Beiheft vii, 55–7.

241

LIST OF ILLUSTRATIONS

43 Munich, Antikensammlungen 2423, from Vulci. *ARV* 30, 1.

44 Rome, Torlonia Collection 73, from Vulci. *ARV* 30, 2. After *Antike Denkmäler* ii, pl. 8.

45 London, British Museum E 255, from Vulci. *ARV* 31, 2.

46 Brussels, Musées Royaux R 351, from Vulci. *ARV* 31, 7.

47 London, British Museum E 767, from Vulci. *ARV* 31, 6.

48 Athens, Agora Museum P 24113, from Athens. *ARV* 213, 242.

49 Athens, National Museum 1628, from Tanagra. *ARV* 25, 1. After Pfuhl, fig. 386.

50 Berlin, Staatliche Museen 2278, from Vulci. *ARV* 21, 1. After Pfuhl, fig. 418.

51 Gotha, from Kolias. *ARV* 20. After *CVA*.

52 Athens, National Museum, Akr. 2590 and Oxford, Ashmolean Museum 1927.4602, from Athens. *ARV* 1598. After *JHS* lxxvi, pl. 2.1.

53 Athens, Acropolis Museum, Akr. 1037, from Athens. *ARV* 1598.

54 London, British Museum E 437, from Cerveteri. *ARV* 54, 5.

55 Tarquinia, Museo Nazionale RC 6848, from Tarquinia. *ARV* 60, 66.

56 Paris, Louvre G 3. *ARV* 53, 1.

57 London, British Museum E 258, from Vulci. *ARV* 54, 4.

58 Kings Point, Schimmel Collection. *Para* 326, 7 *bis*.

59 Copenhagen, National Museum inv. 13407. *ARV* 59, 57.

60 Oxford, Ashmolean Museum 516, from Vulci. *ARV* 63, 92.

61 Castle Ashby, from Vulci. *ARV* 55, 18.

62 Bologna, Museo Civico 361, from Bologna. *ARV* 65, 113.

63 Basel, Antikenmuseum BS 459. *Para* 327, 50 *bis*.

64 Formerly Arlesheim, Schweizer. *ARV* 57, 42.

65 London, British Museum E 8. *ARV* 63, 88.

66 London, British Museum E 3. *ARV* 70, 3.

67 Arlesheim, Schweizer Collection. *ARV* 1705, 6 *bis*.

68 Oberlin, Allen Art Museum 67.61. *Para* 329, 14 *bis*.

69 Baltimore, John Hopkins University, from Chiusi? *ARV* 75, 56.

70 Athens, National Museum, Akr. 68, from Athens. *ARV* 75, 62. After *Akr. Vasen* ii.

71 Leningrad, Hermitage Museum inv. 14611, from Berezan. *ARV* 75, 60. Beazley drawing.

72 London, British Museum 1929.11–11.1, from Spina. *ARV* 74, 35.

73 London, British Museum E 35, from Vulci. *ARV* 74, 38.

74 Copenhagen, National Museum 119, from Greece. *ARV* 75, 59.

75 London, British Museum E 38, from Vulci. *ARV* 72, 16.

76 Oxford, Ashmolean Museum 520. *ARV* 76, 84.

77 London, British Museum E 135, from Vulci. *ARV* 78, 93.

78 London, British Museum E 137, from Vulci. *ARV* 78, 95.

79 New York, Metropolitan Museum inv. 41.162.8, Rogers Fund. *ARV* 165, 6.

80 London, British Museum E 6, from Vulci. *ARV* 166, 11.

81 Paris, Petit Palais 382, from Athens. *ARV* 81, 1. After Klein, *Lieblingsinschriften* 88.

82 Brunswick, Bowdoin College, from Cerveteri. *ARV* 167, 5.

83 Castle Ashby. *ARV* 172, 1.

84 Brussels, Musées Royaux R 259. *ARV* 169, 7.

85 Winchester College 42. *ARV* 170, 1.

86 Munich, Antikensammlungen 2588, from Vulci. *ARV* 162, 2. After Furtwängler-Reichhold, iii, 240.

87 Rome, Villa Giulia Museum 50590. *ARV* 162, 5.

88 Paris, Louvre G 10. *ARV* 83, 3.

89 Rome, Villa Giulia Museum, from Cerveteri. *ARV* 82, 1.

90 Rome, Villa Giulia Museum 20760, from Cerveteri. *ARV* 83, 14.

91 Paris, Louvre CA 1527, from Tanagra. *ARV* 83, 12.

92 Paris, Louvre G 13. *ARV* 86, a.

93 Castle Ashby, from Vulci. *ARV* 124, 7.

94 Rome, Villa Giulia Museum 27250, from Todi. *ARV* 124, 8. After Hoppin, ii, 305.

95 Melbourne, University 1730.4, from Vulci. *ARV* 125, 20.

96 London, British Museum E 815, from Vulci. *ARV* 125, 15.

97 Rome, Villa Giulia Museum 20749, from Cerveteri. *ARV* 127, 30.

98 Berlin, Staatliche Museen 2324, from Vulci. *ARV* 126, 26. After Pfuhl, fig. 321.

99 Boston, Museum of Fine Arts 95.61, Gift of E. P. Warren, from Vulci. *ARV* 132.

100 Athens, National Museum Akr. 102, from Athens. *ARV* 1625. After *Akr. Vasen* ii.

101 Athens, National Museum Akr. 166, from Athens. *ARV* 92, 64. After *Akr. Vasen* ii.

102 London, British Museum 1920.6–13.1, from Capua. *ARV* 88, 1.

103 Kings Point, Schimmel Collection. See *RA* 1972, 83ff.

104 Maplewood, Noble Collection. *Para* 330.

105 Basel, Antikenmuseum BS 463. *ARV* 147, 16.

106 Munich, Antikensammlungen 2619A, from Vulci. *ARV* 146, 2.

107 London, British Museum B 668, from Marion. *ARV* 98, 1.

108 Cambridge, Fitzwilliam Museum GR 49.1864, from Vulci. *ARV* 111, 14.

109 London, British Museum E 34, from Marion. *ARV* 110, 8.

110 Leningrad, Hermitage Museum 647, from Marion. *ARV* 110, 2.

111 Munich, Antikensammlungen 2589, from Vulci. *ARV* 112, 1.

112 Berlin, Staatliche Museen 3251, from Vulci. *ARV* 113, 7. After *CVA*.

113 Berlin, Staatliche Museen inv. 3232. *ARV* 117, 2.

114 London, British Museum E 43. *ARV* 118, 13.

115 Munich, Antikensammlungen inv. 8771. See *MJBK* xxii, 7ff.

116 Florence, Museo Archeologico 4211. *ARV* 121, 22.

117 London, British Museum E 57, from Vulci. *ARV* 120, 9.

118 Oxford, Ashmolean Museum 303, from Chiusi. *ARV* 120, 7.

119 Boston, Museum of Fine Arts 01.8024, H. L. Pierce Fund, from Orvieto. *ARV* 173, 9.

120 Berlin, Staatliche Museen (East) 2273, from Vulci. *ARV* 174, 31.

121 London, British Museum E 42. *ARV* 174, 20.

122 Athens, Agora Museum P 24102, from Athens. *ARV* 176, 1.

123 Berlin, Staatliche Museen 2269, from Chiusi. *ARV* 177, 1.

124 London, British Museum E 23, from Chiusi. *ARV* 179, 1.

125 Once London, Mitchell Collection, from Greece. *ARV* 178, 5. After *JHS* xvi, pl. 13.

126 New York, Metropolitan Museum 07.286.47, Rogers Fund. *ARV* 175.

127 Once Luzern market. *ARV* 136, 10.

128 Rhodes, Archaeological Museum 13386, from Camirus. *ARV* 139, 23. After *CVA*.

129 Würzburg, Martin von Wagner Museum 507, from Vulci. *ARV* 181, 1. After

Furtwängler-Reichhold, pl, 103.

130 Cambridge, Fogg Art Museum 1960.236. *ARV* 185, 31.

131 Copenhagen, National Museum inv. 13365. *ARV* 185, 32.

132 Munich, Antikensammlungen 2344, from Vulci. *ARV* 182, 6.

133 Tarquinia, Museo Nazionale RC 4196, from Tarquinia. *ARV* 185, 35.

134 Paris, Bibl. Nat. 385 and Bonn, Akademisches Kunstmuseum 143, from Tarquinia. *ARV* 186, 50. Beazley drawing.

135 Naples, Museo Nazionale 2422, from Nola. *ARV* 189, 74.

136 Basel, Wilhelm Collection, from Vulci. *ARV* 189, 73.

137 London, British Museum E 441, from Vulci. *ARV* 187, 57.

138 London, British Museum E 270, from Vulci. *ARV* 183, 15.

139 Florence, Museo Nazionale 4218. *ARV* 191, 102.

140 Harrow School 55. *ARV* 183, 11. After *JHS* xxx, pl. 7.

141 Paris, Louvre CA 453, from Attica. *ARV* 184, 22.

142 Berlin, Staatliche Museen 2170, from Cerveteri. *ARV* 185, 28.

143 Vienna, Kunsthistorisches Museum 3725, from Cerveteri. *ARV* 204, 109. After Pfuhl, fig. 370.

144 Berlin, Staatliche Museen 2160, from Vulci. *ARV* 196, 1.

145 Würzburg, Martin von Wagner Museum 500, from Vulci. *ARV* 197, 8.

146 Basel, Antikenmuseum BS 456. *ARV* 1634, *Para* 342, 1 *bis*.

147 Oxford, Ashmolean Museum 1927.4502. *ARV* 210, 172.

148 Munich, Antikensammlungen inv. 8766. *ARV* 1700, *Para* 342, 21 *bis*.

149 Basel, Antikenmuseum BS 453. *ARV* 1634, 30 *bis*.

150 Paris, Louvre G 175. *ARV* 206, 124.

151 Munich, Antikensammlungen 2313, from Vulci. *ARV* 198, 12.

152 New York, Metropolitan Museum 56.171.38, from Nola. *ARV* 197, 3. Beazley drawing.

153 Munich, Antikensammlungen 2312, from Vulci. *ARV* 197, 11.

154 Karlsruhe, Badisches Landesmuseum 68. 101. *Para* 344, 131 *bis*.

155 Paris, Louvre G 192, from Vulci. *ARV* 208, 160.

156 London, British Museum E 162, from Vulci. *ARV* 209, 165.

157 Rome, Vatican Museums, from Vulci. *ARV* 209, 166.

158 Vienna, Kunsthistorisches Museum 741. *ARV* 203, 101. After *CVA*.

159 Palermo, Museo Nazionale V 669, from Gela. *ARV* 211, 188.

160 Switzerland, private. *ARV* 202, 77.

161 Berlin, Staatliche Museen 1965.5. *Para* 345, 184 *bis*.

162 Boston, Museum of Fine Arts 95.19, C. P. Perkins Fund. *ARV* 220, 5.

163 Munich, Antikensammlungen 2381, from S. Italy. *ARV* 221, 14.

164 Brussels, Musées Royaux A 721. *ARV* 226, 5.

165 Hamburg, Museum für Kunst und Gewerbe 1966.34. *Para* 347, 8 *ter*.

166 Paris, Louvre G 163, from Cerveteri. *ARV* 227, 12.

167 Cambridge, Fitzwilliam Museum GR 18.1937. *ARV* 231, 76.

168 Athens, National Museum Akr. 806, from Athens. *ARV* 240, 42. After *Akr. Vasen* ii.

169 Paris, Louvre CA 1947, from Orvieto. *ARV* 240, 44.

170 Naples, Museo Nazionale 2410, from Ruvo. *ARV* 239, 18.

171 Paris, Louvre G 197, from Vulci. *ARV* 238, 1.

172 London, British Museum F. 458. *ARV* 239, 16.

173 Berlin, Staatliche Museen 2162, from Vulci. *ARV* 273, 25.

174 Caltanissetta, from Sabucina. *Para* 354, 39 *bis*. See *AK* xii, 16ff.

175 Maplewood, Noble Collection, from Vulci. *ARV* 276, 70.

176 Paris, Petit Palais 307, from Capua. *ARV* 279, 2.

177 Boston, Museum of Fine Arts 98.882, from Capua. *ARV* 279, 7. Beazley drawing.

178 Paris, Louvre G 220. *ARV* 280, 11. Beazley drawing.

179 Boston, Museum of Fine Arts 64.2032. *ARV* 285, 2; *Para* 355.

180 Paris, Louvre G 536, from Nola. *ARV* 286, 14.

181 Munich, Antikensammlungen 2382, from Sicily. *ARV* 287, 27.

182 Rome, Villa Giulia Museum 48238, from Cerveteri. *ARV* 284, 1.

183 Leningrad, Hermitage Museum 614. *ARV* 288, 11.

184 London, British Museum E 440, from Vulci. *ARV* 289, 1.

185 Stockholm, Medelhavsmuseet 1963.1. *ARV* 1643, 33 *bis*.

186 Boston, Museum of Fine Arts 97.368, from Vulci. *ARV* 290, 1. After *Boston* ii, pl. 36.

187 London, British Museum E 165, from Vulci. *ARV* 294, 62.

188 Copenhagen, National Museum 126. *ARV* 297, 11.

189 New York, Metropolitan Museum 56.171.53, Fletcher Fund, from Vulci. *ARV* 297, 14.

190 London, British Museum 99.7–21.4, from Vulci. *ARV* 297, 15.

191 Munich, Antikensammlungen 2303, from Agrigento. *ARV* 245, 1.

192 Boston, Museum of Fine Arts 13.200, from Gela? *ARV* 247, 1. After *Boston* ii, pl. 34.

193 Leningrad, Hermitage Museum, from Kerch. *ARV* 248, 1. Beazley drawing.

194 London, British Museum E 261, from Vulci. *ARV* 248, 2.

195 Copenhagen, National Museum inv. 3293, from Orvieto. *ARV* 251, 36. After *Mon. Ined.* xi, pl. 50.

196 Brussels, Musées Royaux R 303, from Vulci. *ARV* 249, 6.

197 Paris, Niarchos Collection. *ARV* 250, 18.

198 Palermo, Museo Nazionale V 763, from Chiusi. *ARV* 251, 34.

199 Würzburg, Martin von Wagner Museum 515. *ARV* 256, 5.

200 London, British Museum E 163, from Vulci. *ARV* 258, 26.

201 London, British Museum E 442, from Vulci. *ARV* 257, 9.

202 New York, private. *ARV* 260, 15.

203 Bologna, Museo Civico PU 283, from Orvieto. *ARV* 260, 8.

204 Rome, Villa Giulia 866, from Falerii. *ARV* 264, 67.

205 Private. *Para* 353, 1.

206 Private. *Para* 353, 2.

207 London, British Museum E 510, from Vulci. *ARV* 307, 8. After *JHS* xxxiii, pl. 9.

208 London, British Museum B 674, from Tanagra. *ARV* 267, 1.

209 New York, Metropolitan Museum 21.131, Gift of G. M. A. Richter. *ARV* 269, 1.

210 Cambridge, Fogg Art Museum 1925.30.51. *ARV* 302, 21.

211 Boston, Museum of Fine Arts 13.195, from Gela. *ARV* 35, 1.

212 Paris, Petit Palais 315, from Nola. *ARV* 307, 11.

213 Oxford, Ashmolean Museum 1917.58. *ARV* 309, 14.

214 Berlin, Staatliche Museen 2279, from Vulci. *ARV* 115, 2.

215 Bareiss Collection (New York L.1971.61). See *Harvard Stud. Class. Phil.* lxxvi, 271ff.

216 Athens, National Museum Akr. 432, from Athens. *ARV* 332, 27. After *Akr. Vasen* ii.

217 Eleusis Museum 618, from Eleusis. *ARV* 314, 3.

218 Munich, Antikensammlungen 2645, from Vulci. *ARV* 371, 15. See also [256].

219 London, British Museum E 816, from Vulci. *ARV* 315, 2. Beazley drawing.

220 Munich, Antikensammlungen 2636, from Vulci. *ARV* 317, 16. After Hartwig, *Meisterschalen* pl. 15.1.

221 Basel, Cahn Collection. *ARV* 316, 3.

222 London, British Museum E 44, from Vulci. *ARV* 318, 2.

223 Paris, Louvre G 104, from Cerveteri. *ARV* 318, 1.

224 Brussels, Musées Royaux A 889, from Chiusi. *ARV* 329, 130.

225 Brunswick, Bowdoin College 1930.1 (+fr. given by D. von Bothmer), from Cerveteri. *ARV* 328, 114.

226 Boston, Museum of Fine Arts 63.873. *Para* 360, 74 *quater*.

227 Munich, Antikensammlungen 2637, from Vulci. *ARV* 322, 28.

228 Paris, Louvre G 105, from Vulci. *ARV* 324, 60.

229 Kings Point, Schimmel Collection. *ARV* 329, 125 *bis*.

230 Basel, Antikenmuseum BS 439. *ARV* 323, 56.

231 New York, Metropolitan Museum 12.231.2, from Cerveteri. *ARV* 319, 6. After Richter and Hall.

232 Perugia, Museo Civico 89, from Vulci. *ARV* 320, 8. After Hartwig, *Meisterschalen* pl. 58.

233 Basel, Antikenmuseum BS 440. *ARV* 326, 86 *bis*; *Para* 359.

234 Berlin, Staatliche Museen (East) 2322, from Vulci. *ARV* 329, 134.

235 Once Berlin, Staatliche Museen inv. 3139, from Italy. *ARV* 321, 23. After Pfuhl, fig. 408.

236 Oxford, Ashmolean Museum 300, from Chiusi. *ARV* 357, 69

237 Basel, Antikenmuseum BS 438, from Vulci. *ARV* 351, 8.

238 Paris, Louvre G 135, from Vulci. *ARV* 355, 45.

239 Berlin, Staatliche Museen (East) 2325, from Pomarico. *ARV* 335, 1.

240 Baltimore, Walters Art Gallery 48.2115. *ARV* 336, 16.

241 Once Munich, Arndt Collection. *ARV* 339, 55.

242 Houston, de Ménil Collection. *ARV* 1646, 85 *bis*.

243 Berlin, Staatliche Museen 2303, from Vulci. *ARV* 336, 10.

244 London, British Museum 1901.5–14.1, from Orvieto. *ARV* 348, 2.

245 Paris, Louvre G 152, from Vulci. *ARV* 369, 1.

246 Bareiss Collection (New York L.69.11.35). *Para* 367, 1 *bis*.

247 London, British Museum E 69, from Vulci. *ARV* 369, 2.

248 Vienna, Kunsthistorisches Museum inv. 3710, from Cerveteri. *ARV* 380, 171. After Furtwängler-Reichhold, pl. 84.

249 New York, Metropolitan Museum 25.189.1, from Gela. *ARV* 384, 211.

250 Berlin, Staatliche Museen (East) 2301, from Tarquinia. *ARV* 378, 129.

251 Rome, Vatican Museums, from Vulci. *ARV* 369, 6.

252 London, British Museum E 65, from Capua. *ARV* 370, 13.

253 London, British Museum E 68, from Vulci. *ARV* 371, 24.

254 Würzburg, Martin von Wagner Museum 479, from Vulci. *ARV* 372, 32.

255 Paris, Bibliothèque Nationale 576. *ARV* 371, 14.

256 Munich, Antikensammlungen 2645, from Vulci. *ARV* 371, 15. See also [*218*].

257 Warsaw, National Museum. *ARV* 382, 185. After *VPol.*

258 Leningrad, Hermitage Museum 679. *ARV* 382, 188.

259 Boston, Museum of Fine Arts 10.176, from Greece. *ARV* 381, 173.

260 Oxford, Ashmolean Museum 1967.304, from Vulci. *ARV* 378, 137

261 Munich, Antikensammlungen 2416, from Agrigento. *ARV* 385, 228.

262 Berlin, Staatliche Museen 2294, from Vulci. *ARV* 400, 1.

263 London, British Museum E 78, from Vulci. *ARV* 401, 3.

264 Munich, Antikensammlungen 2650, from Vulci. *ARV* 401, 2.

265 Cambridge, Corpus Christi. *ARV* 402, 12.

266 Cambridge, Fogg Art Museum 1927.149. *ARV* 402, 16.

267 London, British Museum D 13, from Locri? *ARV* 403, 38.

268 Munich, Antikensammlungen 2640, from Vulci. *ARV* 402, 22.

269 Tarquinia, Museo Nazionale RC 5291, from Tarquinia. *ARV* 405, 1. After *Mon. Ined.* xi, pl. 20.

270 London, British Museum E 76, from Vulci. *ARV* 406, 1.

271 London, British Museum E 75, from Vulci. *ARV* 406, 2. After Hartwig, *Meisterschalen* pl. 43.

272 Oxford, Ashmolean Museum 1967.305, from Cerveteri. *ARV* 408, 37.

273 Ruvo, Museo Jatta 1539, from Ruvo. *ARV* 408, 33.

274 Boston, Museum of Fine Arts 63.1246, W. F. Warden Fund. *Para* 373, 34 *quater*.

275 Berlin, Staatliche Museen 2309, from Capua. *Para* 372, 11 *bis*.

276 Leningrad, Hermitage Museum 653. *ARV* 413, 23.

277 Zürich, University Museum. *Para* 373, 34 *bis*.

278 Oxford, Ashmolean Museum 305. *ARV* 416, 3.

279 Roman market, from Vulci. *ARV* 417, 4. Gerhard, *AV* pl. 166.

280 Paris, Bibliothèque Nationale 573, from Vulci. *ARV* 417, 1.

281 Vienna, Kunsthistorisches Museum 3694, from Cerveteri. *ARV* 427, 3. After Furtwängler-Reichhold, pl. 53.

282 Athens, National Museum TE 556, from Athens. *Para* 376, 273 *bis*.

283 Baltimore, Johns Hopkins University, from Chiusi. *ARV* 442, 215.

284 Rome, Vatican Museums, from Vulci. *ARV* 427, 2.

285 Vienna, Kunsthistorisches Museum 3695, from Cerveteri. *ARV* 429, 26.

286 Basel, Antikenmuseum Käppeli 425. *ARV* 430, 31.

287 London, British Museum E 48, from Vulci. *ARV* 431, 47.

288 Rome, Vatican Museums, from Cerveteri. *ARV* 437, 116.

289 Berlin, Staatliche Museen 2285, from Cerveteri. *ARV* 431, 48.

290 London, British Museum E 49, from Vulci. *ARV* 432, 52.

291 London, British Museum E 54, from Vulci. *ARV* 436, 96.

292 Paris, Louvre G 115, from Capua. *ARV* 434, 74.

293 Berlin, Staatliche Museen 2289, from Vulci. *ARV* 435, 95.

294 Cleveland Museum of Art 66.114, L. C. Hanna Bequest. *Para* 376, 266 *bis*.

295 Paris, Bibliothèque Nationale 542, from Vulci. *ARV* 438, 133.

296 Munich, Antikensammlungen 2646, from Vulci. *ARV* 437, 128.

297 Boston, Museum of Fine Arts 1970.233. *ARV* 444, 241.

298 Brussels, Musées Royaux A 718. *ARV* 445, 256.

299 London, British Museum E 768, from Cerveteri. *ARV* 446, 262.

300 Rome, Vatican Museums, from Vulci. *ARV* 449, 2.

301 Rome, Vatican Museums, from Vulci. *ARV* 451, 1.

302 Tarquinia, Museo Nazionale, from Tarquinia. *ARV* 367, 94.

303 Edinburgh, Royal Scottish Museum 1887.213, from Italy. *ARV* 364, 46.

304 Switzerland, private. *ARV* 361, 7.

305 Berlin, Staatliche Museen 2298, from Vulci. *ARV* 364, 52.

306 Leningrad, Hermitage Museum 637, from Cerveteri. *ARV* 360, 1.

307 Munich, Antikensammlungen 2314, from Vulci. *ARV* 362, 14.

308 Boston, Museum of Fine Arts 13.186, F. Bartlett Donation, from Suessula. *ARV* 458, 1.

309 London, British Museum E 140, from Capua. *ARV* 459, 3.

310 Berlin, Staatliche Museen 2291, from Vulci. *ARV* 459, 4.

311 Berlin, Staatliche Museen 2290, from Vulci. *ARV* 462, 48.

312 Rome, Villa Giulia Museum 50396, from Cerveteri? *ARV* 465, 82.

313 Munich, Antikensammlungen 2654, from Vulci. *ARV* 462, 47.

314 Munich, Antikensammlungen 2657, from Vulci. *ARV* 475, 267.

315 Lausanne, private. *ARV* 471, 185.

316 Brunswick, Bowdoin College 23.30. *ARV* 480, 339.

317 London, British Museum E 61, from Vulci. *ARV* 468, 145.

318 Oxford, Ashmolean Museum 1929.175, from Athens. *ARV* 480, 337.

319 Cambridge, Fitzwilliam Museum GR 22.1937. *ARV* 565, 36.

320 Cleveland Museum of Art 24.197, Mrs L. C. Hanna Gift. *ARV* 564, 18.

321 Cambridge, Fogg Museum of Art 60.346, from Agrigento. *ARV* 563, 8. Beazley drawing.

322 Boston, Museum of Fine Arts 10.191. *ARV* 569, 49. After *Boston* iii, pl. 85.

323 Milan, Torno Collection, from Ruvo. *ARV* 571, 73. See *JHS* lxxxi, pls. 6, 7.

324 Munich, Antikensammlungen 2323, from Vulci. *ARV* 571, 72.

325 Boston, Museum of Fine Arts 03.788. *ARV* 571, 75. After *Boston* iii, pl. 86.

326 London, British Museum 1920.3–15.3, from Capua. *ARV* 571, 79.

327 Boston, Museum of Fine Arts 08.417, from Capua. *ARV* 579, 84. After *Boston* iii, pl. 86.

328 London, British Museum E 171, from Camirus. *ARV* 579, 87.

329 London, British Museum E 182, from Vulci. *ARV* 580, 2.

330 Berlin, Staatliche Museen 2172, from Etruria. *ARV* 581, 4.

331 Basel, Borowski Collection. See *AJA* lxxiv, 331ff.

332 London, British Museum E 363, from Camirus. *ARV* 586, 36.

333 Basel, Antikenmuseum BS 415. See *AK* x, 70ff.

334 Boston, Museum of Fine Arts 13.199, F. Bartlett Fund, from Gela. *ARV* 588, 73.

335 Boston, Museum of Fine Arts 10.185, from Cumae. *ARV* 550, 1.

336 Athens, National Museum 9683, from Boeotia. *ARV* 554, 82.

337 Athens, National Museum Akr. 760, from Athens *ARV* 552, 20. After *Akr. Vasen* ii.

338 Munich, Antikensammlungen 2417, from Agrigento. *ARV* 556, 101.

339 Boston, Museum of Fine Arts 10.184, from Suessula. *ARV* 553, 39.

340 Naples, Museo Nazionale, from Cumae. *ARV* 551, 15. After Pfuhl, fig. 477.

341 London, British Museum E 512, from Vulci. *ARV* 557, 125. After *JHS* xxxii, pl. 8.

342 Berlin, Staatliche Museen (East) inv. 3206, from Etruria. *ARV* 551, 10.

343 Palermo, Museo Nazionale V 778, from Agrigento. *ARV* 550, 2.

344 Vienna, Kunsthistorisches Museum 3727, from Cerveteri. *ARV* 555, 88.

345 Schwerin Museum 1304, from S. Italy. *ARV* 553, 38.

346 Athens, Serpieri Collection (Vlasto), from Athens. *ARV* 552, 28.

347 Boston, Museum of Fine Arts 13.198, F. Bartlett Donation, from Gela. *ARV* 557, 113.

348 Oxford, Ashmolean Museum 312, from Gela. *ARV* 556, 102.

349 Munich, Antikensammlungen inv. 8725. *ARV* 554, 85.

350 Munich, Antikensammlungen 2413, from Vulci. *ARV* 495, 1. After Furtwängler-Reichhold, pl. 137.

351 Rome, Vatican Museums, from Vulci. *ARV* 484, 21.

352 Rome, Villa Giulia Museum, from Cerveteri. *ARV* 485, 33.

353 Palermo, Museo Nazionale V 672, from Gela. *ARV* 490, 119.

354 Paris, Louvre G 416, from Nola. *ARV* 484, 17.

355 London, British Museum E 410, from Vulci. *ARV* 494, 1.

356 Oxford, Ashmolean Museum 1925.68, from Gela. *ARV* 641, 87.

357 Oxford, Ashmolean Museum 277, from Gela. *ARV* 636, 22.
358 Palermo, Museo Nazionale V 676, from Gela. *ARV* 641, 83.
359 London, British Museum E 303, from Gela. *ARV* 636, 4. Beazley drawing.
360 Berlin, Staatliche Museen (East) 2331. *ARV* 646, 7.
361 Cleveland Museum of Art 28.660, C. W. Harkness Fund, from Italy. *ARV* 648, 37.
362 Bern, Historisches Museum 12215, from Nola. *ARV* 646, 3.
363 Paris, Louvre G 210, from Capua. *ARV* 647, 18.
364 Boston, Museum of Fine Arts 68.163, L. T. Clay Gift. *Para* 402.
365 Brussels, Musées Royaux A 1019, from Eretria. *ARV* 652, 3.

366 London, British Museum E 299, from Nola. *ARV* 650, 1. Beazley drawing.
367 Boston, Museum of Fine Arts 76.46, from Capua. *ARV* 654, 13. After *Boston* ii, pl. 45.
368 Basel market. *Para* 417.
369 Paris, Louvre CA 2259, from Kerch. *ARV* 797, 137.
370 Berlin, Staatliche Museen inv. 31426. *ARV* 795, 100.
371 Copenhagen, National Museum inv. 6, from Nola. *ARV* 787, 3.
372 Leningrad, Hermitage Museum 823, from Nola. *ARV* 787, 5.
373 Oxford, Ashmolean Museum 517. *ARV* 785, 8.
374 Oxford, Ashmolean Museum 1927.71. *ARV* 790, 16.
375 London, British Museum E 772, from Athens. *ARV* 806, 90. After Furtwängler-Reichhold, pl. 57.2.

376 London, British Museum E 66, from Nola. *ARV* 808, 2.
377 Paris, Louvre CA 2183. *ARV* 813, 96.
378 Boston, Museum of Fine Arts 98.931, from Etruria. *ARV* 817, 2. After *Boston* iii, pl. 88.
379 Boston, Museum of Fine Arts 95.28, from Vulci. *ARV* 816, 1. After Pfuhl, fig. 449.
380 Boston, Museum of Fine Arts 95.30. *ARV* 819, 44. After *Boston* iii, pl. 91.
381 Leningrad, Hermitage Museum 658, from Orvieto. *ARV* 817, 3.
382 Boston, Museum of Fine Arts 10.572. *ARV* 821, 5. After *Boston* iii, pl. 87.
383 Ferrara, Museo Nazionale di Spina T. 867, from Spina. *ARV* 205, 114.

HEAD DETAILS IN TEXT

Andokides Painter (p. 16) *ARV* nos. 2*bis*, 2*bis*, 2*bis*, 8, 9; Euphronios (p. 32) *ARV* nos. 3*bis*, 5, 17, 21, 7; Euthymides (p. 34) *ARV* nos. 1, 1, 3, 4, 8; Oltos (p. 57) *ARV* nos. 6, 93, 91, 5, 66; Epiktetos (p. 58) *ARV* nos. 3, 15, 63, 94, 86; Kleophrades Painter (p. 93) *ARV* nos. 103, 104, 6, 3; Berlin Painter (p. 95) *ARV* nos. 1, 1*bis*, 164, 141, 21*bis*; Onesimos (p. 134) *ARV* nos. 9, 14, 74, 107, 76; Brygos Painter (p. 136) *ARV* nos. 135, 48, 2, 24, 203; Douris (p. 138) *ARV* nos. 89, 19, 4, 16, 141; Pan Painter (p. 181) *ARV* nos. 1, 1, 115, 21, (near) 5. The fragment on p. 10 is in the author's collection.

The drawing on p. 209 is by Marion Cox.

Dimensions of some complete vases are given in centimetres in the captions.

The author and publishers are deeply grateful to the many museums and collectors named in the above list for their kindness in supplying photographs and granting permission to publish them. The following other sources of photographs are also gratefully acknowledged: Max Hirmer [*3, 11, 23–4, 26, 32, 34, 38, 40–3, 55–6, 66, 77–8, 90, 132, 135, 141, 144, 150–1, 153, 157, 159, 170–1, 181, 191, 198, 218, 222–4, 227, 245, 256, 261, 268, 280, 288, 292–3, 295–6, 298, 312, 338, 343, 345, 350, 353–4, 383*]; Professor Bloesch [*277*]; Professor Trendall [*95*]; German Institute, Rome [*273, 302, 352, 358*]; Photo Bulloz (Petit Palais); Photo Chuzeville (Louvre); Robert L. Wilkins (Castle Ashby); Ist. Cent. del Restauro, Rome [*20*]. The Beazley drawings are from the Beazley Archive in Oxford.

INDEX OF ARTISTS AND GROUPS

Principal page references are **bold**. Figure numbers are *italicised*

P. = Painter; (p) = potter

INDEX OF MYTHOLOGICAL SUBJECTS

Index to text of Chapter Eight only; and select figure numbers *italicised*

GENERAL INDEX

(k) = kalos